Ten Documents That Created America

Ten Documents That Created America

MINT EDITIONS

Ten Documents That Created America features work first published between 1776 and 1871.

This edition published by Mint Editions 2023.

ISBN 9798888975350 | E-ISBN 9798888975503

Published by Mint Editions®

MINT EDITIONS

minteditionbooks.com

Publishing Director: Katie Connolly
Design: Ponderosa Pine Design
Production and Project Management: Micaela Clark
Typesetting: Westchester Publishing Services

Contents

Common Sense	9
The Declaration of Independence	63
The Articles of Confederation	67
The United States' Constitution by Founding Fathers	77
The United States Bill of Rights	94
Indian Removal Act of 1830	97
The Indian Appropriations Act	99
What to the Slave is the Fourth of July	123
The Emancipation Proclamation	150
General Order No. 3	153
The Indian Appropriations Act (Continued)	154

"The mere imparting of information is not education. Above all things, the effort must result in making a man think."

—Dr. Carter G. Woodson, *The Mis-Education of the Negro*

Common Sense

Of the Origin and Design of Government in General, with Concise Remarks on the English Constitution

Some writers have so confounded society with government, as to leave little or no distinction between them; whereas they are not only different, but have different origins. Society is produced by our wants, and government by our wickedness; the former promotes our happiness *positively* by uniting our affections, the latter *negatively* by restraining our vices. The one encourages intercourse, the other creates distinctions. The first a patron, the last a punisher.

Society in every state is a blessing, but government even in its best state is but a necessary evil; in its worst state an intolerable one; for when we suffer, or are exposed to the same miseries *by a government*, which we might expect in a country *without government*, our calamity is heightened by reflecting that we furnish the means by which we suffer. Government, like dress, is the badge of lost innocence; the palaces of kings are built on the ruins of the bowers of paradise. For were the impulses of conscience clear, uniform, and irresistibly obeyed, man would need no other lawgiver; but that not being the case, he finds it necessary to surrender up a part of his property to furnish means for the protection of the rest; and this he is induced to do by the same prudence which in every other case advises him out of two evils to choose the least. *Wherefore*, security being the true design and end of government, it unanswerably follows that whatever *form* thereof appears most likely to ensure it to us, with the least expence and greatest benefit, is preferable to all others.

In order to gain a clear and just idea of the design and end of government, let us suppose a small number of persons settled in some sequestered part of the earth, unconnected with the rest, they will then represent the first peopling of any country, or of the world. In this state of natural liberty, society will be their first thought. A thousand motives will excite them thereto, the strength of one man is so unequal to his wants, and his mind so unfitted for perpetual solitude, that he is soon obliged to seek assistance and relief of another, who in his turn requires the same. Four or five united would be able to raise a tolerable dwelling in the midst of a wilderness, but *one* man might labour out of the common period of life without accomplishing anything; when he had felled his timber he could not remove it, nor erect it after it was removed; hunger in the mean time would urge him from his work, and every different want call him a different way. Disease, nay even misfortune would be death, for though neither might be mortal, yet either would disable him from living, and reduce him to a state in which he might rather be said to perish than to die.

Thus necessity, like a gravitating power, would soon form our newly arrived emigrants into society, the reciprocal blessings of which, would supersede, and render the obligations of law and government unnecessary while they remained perfectly just to each other; but as nothing but heaven is impregnable to vice, it will unavoidably happen, that in proportion as they surmount the first difficulties of emigration, which bound them together in a common cause, they will begin to relax in their duty and attachment to each other; and this remissness, will point out the necessity, of establishing some form of government to supply the defect of moral virtue.

Some convenient tree will afford them a State-House, under the branches of which, the whole colony may assemble to deliberate on public matters. It is more than probable that their first laws will have the title only of *regulations*, and be enforced by no other penalty than public disesteem. In this first parliament every man, by natural right, will have a seat.

But as the colony increases, the public concerns will increase likewise, and the distance at which the members may be separated, will render it too inconvenient for all of them to meet on every occasion as at first, when their number was small, their habitations near, and the public concerns few and trifling. This will point out the convenience of their consenting to leave the legislative part to be managed by a select number chosen from the whole body, who are supposed to have the same concerns at stake which those who appointed them, and who will act in the same manner as the whole body would act were they present. If the colony continue increasing, it will become necessary to augment the number of the representatives, and that the interest of every part of the colony may be attended to, it will be found best to divide the whole into convenient parts, each part sending its proper number; and that the *elected* might never form to themselves an interest separate from the *electors*, prudence will point out the propriety of having elections often; because as the *elected* might by that means return and mix again with the general body of the *electors* in a few months, their fidelity to the public will be secured by the prudent reflexion of not making a rod for themselves. And as this frequent interchange will establish a common interest with every part of the community, they will mutually and naturally support each other, and on this (not on the unmeaning name of king) depends the *strength of government, and the happiness of the governed.*

Here then is the origin and rise of government; namely, a mode rendered necessary by the inability of moral virtue to govern the world; here too is the design and end of government, viz. freedom and security. And however our eyes may be dazzled with show, or our ears deceived by sound; however prejudice may warp our wills, or interest darken our understanding, the simple voice of nature and of reason will say, it is right.

I draw my idea of the form of government from a principle in nature, which no art can overturn, viz. that the more simple anything is, the less liable it is to be disordered; and the easier repaired when disordered; and with this maxim in view, I offer a few remarks on the so much boasted constitution of England. That it was noble for the dark and slavish times in which it was erected, is granted. When the world was over run with tyranny the least remove therefrom was a glorious rescue. But that it is imperfect, subject to convulsions, and incapable of producing what it seems to promise, is easily demonstrated.

Absolute governments (tho' the disgrace of human nature) have this advantage with them, that they are simple; if the people suffer, they know the head from which their suffering springs, know likewise the remedy, and are not bewildered by a variety of causes and cures. But the constitution of England is so exceedingly complex, that the nation may suffer for years together without being able to discover in which part the fault lies, some will say in one and some in another, and every political physician will advise a different medicine.

I know it is difficult to get over local or long standing prejudices, yet if we will suffer ourselves to examine the component parts of the English constitution, we shall find them to be the base remains of two ancient tyrannies, compounded with some new republican materials.

First.—The remains of monarchical tyranny in the person of the king.

Secondly.—The remains of aristocratical tyranny in the persons of the peers.

Thirdly.—The new republican materials, in the persons of the commons, on whose virtue depends the freedom of England.

The two first, by being hereditary, are independent of the people; wherefore in a *constitutional sense* they contribute nothing towards the freedom of the state.

To say that the constitution of England is a *union* of three powers reciprocally *checking* each other, is farcical, either the words have no meaning, or they are flat contradictions.

To say that the commons is a check upon the king, presupposes two things:

First.—That the king is not to be trusted without being looked after, or in other words, that a thirst for absolute power is the natural disease of monarchy.

Secondly.—That the commons, by being appointed for that purpose, are either wiser or more worthy of confidence than the crown.

But as the same constitution which gives the commons a power to check the king by withholding the supplies, gives afterwards the king a power to check the commons, by empowering him to reject their other bills; it again supposes that the king is wiser than those whom it has already supposed to be wiser than him. A mere absurdity!

There is something exceedingly ridiculous in the composition of monarchy; it first excludes a man from the means of information, yet empowers him to act in cases where the highest judgment is required. The state of a king shuts him from the world, yet the business of a king requires him to know it thoroughly; wherefore the different parts, by unnaturally opposing and destroying each other, prove the whole character to be absurd and useless.

Some writers have explained the English constitution thus; the king, say they, is one, the people another; the peers are an house in behalf of the king; the commons in behalf of the people; but this hath all the distinctions of a house divided against itself; and though the expressions be pleasantly arranged, yet when examined they appear idle and ambiguous; and it will always happen, that the nicest construction that words are capable of, when applied to the description of something which either cannot exist, or is too incomprehensible to be within the compass of description, will be words of sound only, and though they may amuse the ear, they cannot inform the mind, for this explanation includes a previous question, viz. *How came the king by a power which the people are afraid to trust, and always obliged to check?* Such a power could not be the gift of a wise people, neither can any power, *which needs checking*, be from God; yet the provision, which the constitution makes, supposes such a power to exist.

But the provision is unequal to the task; the means either cannot or will not accomplish the end, and the whole affair is a felo de se; for as the greater weight will always carry up the less, and as all the wheels of a machine are put in motion by one, it only remains to know which power in the constitution has the most weight, for that will govern; and though the others, or a part of them, may clog, or, as the phrase is, check the rapidity of its motion, yet so long as they cannot stop it, their endeavors will be ineffectual; the first moving power will at last have its way, and what it wants in speed is supplied by time.

That the crown is this overbearing part in the English constitution needs not be mentioned, and that it derives its whole consequence merely from being the giver of places and pensions is self-evident, wherefore, though we have been wise enough to shut and lock a door against absolute monarchy, we at the same time have been foolish enough to put the crown in possession of the key.

The prejudice of Englishmen, in favour of their own government by king, lords and commons, arises as much or more from national pride than reason. Individuals are undoubtedly safer in England than in someother countries, but the *will* of the king is as much the *law* of the land in Britain as in France, with this difference, that instead of proceeding directly from his mouth, it is handed to the people under the more formidable shape of an act of parliament. For the fate of Charles the first, hath only made kings more subtle—not more just.

Wherefore, laying aside all national pride and prejudice in favour of modes and forms, the plain truth is, that *it is wholly owing to the constitution of the people, and not to the constitution of the government* that the crown is not as oppressive in England as in Turkey.

An inquiry into the *constitutional errors* in the English form of government is at this time highly necessary, for as we are never in a proper condition of doing justice to others, while we continue under the influence of some leading partiality, so neither are we capable of doing it to ourselves while we remain fettered by any obstinate prejudice. And as a man, who is attached to a prostitute, is unfitted to choose or judge of a wife, so any prepossession in favour of a rotten constitution of government will disable us from discerning a good one.

Of Monarchy and Hereditary Succession

Mankind being originally equals in the order of creation, the equality could only be destroyed by some subsequent circumstance; the distinctions of rich, and poor, may in a great measure be accounted for, and that without having recourse to the harsh ill sounding names of oppression and avarice. Oppression is often the *consequence*, but seldom or never the *means* of riches; and though avarice will preserve a man from being necessitously poor, it generally makes him too timorous to be wealthy.

But there is another and greater distinction for which no truly natural or religious reason can be assigned, and that is, the distinction of men into KINGS and SUBJECTS. Male and female are the distinctions of nature, good and bad the distinctions of heaven; but how a race of men came into the world so exalted above the rest, and distinguished like some new species, is worth enquiring into, and whether they are the means of happiness or of misery to mankind.

In the early ages of the world, according to the scripture chronology, there were no kings; the consequence of which was there were no wars; it is the pride of kings which throw mankind into confusion. Holland without a king hath enjoyed more peace for this last century than any of the monarchial governments in Europe. Antiquity favors the same remark; for the quiet and rural lives of the first patriarchs hath a happy something in them, which vanishes away when we come to the history of Jewish royalty.

Government by kings was first introduced into the world by the Heathens, from whom the children of Israel copied the custom. It was the most prosperous invention the Devil ever set on foot for the promotion of idolatry. The Heathens paid divine honors to their deceased kings, and the christian world hath improved on the plan by doing the same to their living ones. How impious is the title of sacred majesty applied to a worm, who in the midst of his splendor is crumbling into dust!

As the exalting one man so greatly above the rest cannot be justified on the equal rights of nature, so neither can it be defended on the authority of scripture; for the will of the Almighty, as declared by Gideon and the prophet Samuel, expressly disapproves of government by kings. All anti-monarchical parts of scripture have been very smoothly glossed over in monarchical governments, but they undoubtedly merit the attention of countries which have their governments yet to form. "*Render unto Cæsar the things which are Cæsar's*" is the scripture doctrine of courts, yet it is no support of monarchical government, for the Jews at that time were without a king, and in a state of vassalage to the Romans.

Near three thousand years passed away from the Mosaic account of the creation, till the Jews under a national delusion requested a king. Till then their form of government (except in extraordinary cases, where the Almighty interposed) was a kind of republic administred by a judge and the elders of the tribes. Kings they had none, and it was held sinful to acknowledge any being under that title but the Lord of Hosts. And when a man seriously reflects on the idolatrous homage which is paid to the persons of Kings, he need not wonder, that the Almighty ever jealous of his honor, should disapprove of a form of government which so impiously invades the prerogative of heaven.

Monarchy is ranked in scripture as one of the sins of the Jews, for which a curse in reserve is denounced against them. The history of that transaction is worth attending to.

The children of Israel being oppressed by the Midianites, Gideon marched against them with a small army, and victory, thro' the divine interposition, decided in his favour. The Jews elate with success, and attributing it to the generalship of Gideon, proposed making him a king, saying, *Rule thou over us, thou and thy son and thy son's son.* Here was temptation in its fullest extent; not a kingdom only, but an hereditary one, but Gideon in the piety of his soul replied, *I will not rule over you, neither shall my son rule over you. The Lord shall rule over you.* Words need not be more explicit; Gideon doth not *decline* the honor, but denieth their right to give it; neither doth he compliment them with invented declarations of his thanks, but in the positive stile of a prophet charges them with disaffection to their proper Sovereign, the King of heaven.

About one hundred and thirty years after this, they fell again into the same error. The hankering which the Jews had for the idolatrous customs of the Heathens, is something exceedingly unaccountable; but so it was, that laying hold of the misconduct of Samuel's two sons, who were entrusted with some secular concerns, they came in an abrupt and clamorous manner to Samuel, saying, *Behold thou art old, and thy sons walk not in thy ways, now make us a king to judge us like all other nations.* And here we cannot but observe that their motives were bad, viz. that they might be *like* unto other nations, i.e. the Heathens, whereas their true glory laid in being as much *unlike* them as possible. *But the thing displeased Samuel when they said, Give us a king to judge us; and Samuel prayed unto the Lord, and the Lord said unto*

Samuel, Hearken unto the voice of the people in all that they say unto thee, for they have not rejected thee, but they have rejected me, that I should not reign over them. According to all the works which they have done since the day that I brought them up out of Egypt, even unto this day; wherewith they have forsaken me and served other Gods; so do they also unto thee. Now therefore hearken unto their voice, howbeit, protest solemnly unto them and shew them the manner of the king that shall reign over them, i.e. not of any particular king, but the general manner of the kings of the earth, whom Israel was so eagerly copying after. And notwithstanding the great distance of time and difference of manners, the character is still in fashion. *And Samuel told all the words of the Lord unto the people, that asked of him a king. And he said, This shall be the manner of the king that shall reign over you; he will take your sons and appoint them for himself, for his chariots, and to be his horsemen, and some shall run before his chariots* (this description agrees with the present mode of impressing men) *and he will appoint him captains over thousands and captains over fifties, and will set them to ear his ground and to reap his harvest, and to make his instruments of war, and instruments of his chariots; and he will take your daughters to be confectionaries, and to be cooks and to be bakers* (this describes the expence and luxury as well as the oppression of kings) *and he will take your fields and your olive yards, even the best of them, and give them to his servants; and he will take the tenth of your feed, and of your vineyards, and give them to his officers and to his servants* (by which we see that bribery, corruption and favoritism are the standing vices of kings) *and he will take the tenth of your men servants, and your maid servants, and your goodliest young men and your asses, and put them to his work; and he will take the tenth of your sheep, and ye shall be his servants, and ye shall cry out in that day because of your king which ye shall have chosen, and the Lord will not hear you in that day*. This accounts for the continuation of monarchy; neither do the characters of the few good kings which have lived since, either sanctify the title, or blot out the sinfulness of the origin; the high encomium given of David takes no notice of him *officially as a king*, but only as a *man* after God's own heart. *Nevertheless the People refused to obey the voice of Samuel, and they said, Nay, but we will have a king over us, that we may be like all the nations, and that our king may judge us, and go out before us, and fight our battles.* Samuel continued to reason with them, but to no purpose; he set before them their ingratitude, but all would not avail; and seeing them fully bent on their folly, he cried out, *I will call unto the Lord, and he shall send thunder and rain* (which then was a punishment, being in the time of wheat harvest) *that ye may perceive and see that your wickedness is great which ye have done in the sight of the Lord, in asking you a king. So Samuel called unto the Lord, and the Lord sent thunder and rain that day, and all the people greatly feared the Lord and Samuel. And all the people said unto Samuel, Pray for thy servants unto the Lord thy God that we die not, for we have added unto our sins this evil, to ask a king.* These portions of scripture are direct and positive. They admit of no equivocal construction. That the Almighty hath here entered his protest against monarchical government is true, or the scripture is false. And a man hath good reason to believe that there is as much of king-craft, as priest-craft, in withholding the scripture from the public in Popish countries. For monarchy in every instance is the Popery of government.

To the evil of monarchy we have added that of hereditary succession; and as the first is a degradation and lessening of ourselves, so the second, claimed as a matter of right, is an insult and an imposition on posterity. For all men being originally equals, no *one* by *birth* could have a right to set up his own family in perpetual preference to all others forever, and though himself might deserve *some* decent degree of honors of his cotemporaries, yet his descendants might be far too unworthy to inherit them. One of the strongest *natural* proofs of the folly of hereditary right in kings, is, that nature disapproves it, otherwise she would not so frequently turn it into ridicule by giving mankind an *ass for a lion*.

Secondly, as no man at first could possess any other public honors than were bestowed upon him, so the givers of those honors could have no power to give away the right of posterity, and though they might say "We choose you for *our* head," they could not, without manifest injustice to their children, say "that your children and your children's children shall reign over *ours* forever." Because such an unwise, unjust, unnatural compact might (perhaps) in the next succession put them under the government of a rogue or a fool. Most wise men, in their private sentiments, have ever treated hereditary right with contempt; yet it is one of those evils, which when once established is not easily removed; many submit from fear, others from superstition, and the more powerful part shares with the king the plunder of the rest.

This is supposing the present race of kings in the world to have had an honorable origin; whereas it is more than probable, that could we take off the dark covering of antiquity, and trace them to their first rise, that we should find the first of them nothing better than the principal ruffian of some restless gang, whose savage manners or pre-eminence in subtility obtained him the title of chief among plunderers; and who by increasing in power, and extending his depredations, over-awed the quiet and defenceless to purchase their safety by frequent contributions. Yet his electors could have no idea of giving hereditary right to his descendants, because such a perpetual exclusion of themselves was incompatible with the free and unrestrained principles they professed to live by. Wherefore, hereditary succession in the early ages of monarchy could not take place as a matter of claim, but as something casual or complimental; but as few or no records were extant in those days, and traditional history stuffed with fables, it was very easy, after the lapse of a few generations, to trump up some superstitious tale, conveniently timed, Mahomet like, to cram hereditary right down the throats of the vulgar. Perhaps the disorders which threatened, or seemed to threaten, on the decease of a leader and the choice of a new one (for elections among ruffians could not be very orderly) induced many at first to favor hereditary pretensions; by which means it happened, as it hath happened since, that what at first was submitted to as a convenience, was afterwards claimed as a right.

England, since the conquest, hath known some few good monarchs, but groaned beneath a much larger number of bad ones; yet no man in his senses can say that their claim under William the Conqueror is a very honorable one. A French bastard landing with an armed banditti, and establishing himself king of England against the consent of the natives, is in plain terms a very paltry rascally original.—It certainly hath no divinity in it. However, it is needless to spend much time in exposing the folly of hereditary right; if there are any so weak as to believe it, let them promiscuously worship the ass and lion, and welcome. I shall neither copy their humility, nor disturb their devotion.

Yet I should be glad to ask how they suppose kings came at first? The question admits but of three answers, viz. either by lot, by election, or by usurpation. If the first king was taken by lot, it establishes a precedent for the next, which excludes hereditary succession. Saul was by lot, yet the succession was not hereditary, neither does it appear from that transaction there was any intention it ever should. If the first king of any country was by election, that likewise establishes a precedent for the next; for to say, that the *right* of all future generations is taken away, by the act of the first electors, in their choice not only of a king, but of a family of kings forever, hath no parrallel in or out of scripture but the doctrine of original sin, which supposes the free will of all men lost in Adam; and from such comparison, and it will admit of no other, hereditary succession can derive no glory. For as in Adam all sinned, and as in the first electors all men obeyed; as in the one all mankind were subjected to Satan, and in the other to Sovereignty; as our innocence was lost in the first, and our authority in the last; and as both disable us from reassuming some former state and privilege, it unanswerably follows that original sin and hereditary succession are parellels. Dishonorable rank! Inglorious connexion! Yet the most subtile sophist cannot produce a juster simile.

As to usurpation, no man will be so hardy as to defend it; and that William the Conqueror was an usurper is a fact not to be contradicted. The plain truth is, that the antiquity of English monarchy will not bear looking into.

But it is not so much the absurdity as the evil of hereditary succession which concerns mankind. Did it ensure a race of good and wise men it would have the seal of divine authority, but as it opens a door to the *foolish*, the *wicked*, and the *improper*, it hath in it the nature of oppression. Men who look upon themselves born to reign, and others to obey, soon grow insolent; selected from the rest of mankind their minds are early poisoned by importance; and the world they act in differs so materially from the world at large, that they have but little opportunity of knowing its true interests, and when they succeed to the government are frequently the most ignorant and unfit of any throughout the dominions.

Another evil which attends hereditary succession is, that the throne is subject to be possessed by a minor at any age; all which time the regency, acting under the cover of a king, have every opportunity and inducement to betray their trust. The same national misfortune happens, when a king worn out with age and infirmity, enters the last stage of human weakness. In both these cases the public becomes a prey to every miscreant, who can tamper successfully with the follies either of age or infancy.

The most plausible plea, which hath ever been offered in favour of hereditary succession, is, that it preserves a nation from civil wars; and were this true, it would be weighty; whereas, it is the most barefaced falsity ever imposed upon mankind. The whole history of England disowns the fact. Thirty kings and two minors have reigned in that distracted kingdom since the conquest, in which time there have been (including the Revolution) no less than eight civil wars and nineteen rebellions. Wherefore instead of making for peace, it makes against it, and destroys the very foundation it seems to stand on.

The contest for monarchy and succession, between the houses of York and Lancaster, laid England in a scene of blood for many years. Twelve pitched battles, besides skirmishes and sieges, were fought between Henry and Edward. Twice was Henry prisoner to Edward, who in his turn was prisoner to Henry. And so uncertain is the fate of war and the temper of a nation, when nothing but personal matters are the ground of a quarrel, that Henry was taken in triumph from a prison to a palace, and Edward obliged to fly from a palace to a foreign land; yet, as sudden transitions of temper are seldom lasting, Henry in his turn was driven from the throne, and Edward recalled to succeed him. The parliament always following the strongest side.

This contest began in the reign of Henry the Sixth, and was not entirely extinguished till Henry the Seventh, in whom the families were united. Including a period of 67 years, viz. from 1422 to 1489.

In short, monarchy and succession have laid (not this or that kingdom only) but the world in blood and ashes. 'Tis a form of government which the word of God bears testimony against, and blood will attend it.

If we inquire into the business of a king, we shall find that in some countries they have none; and after sauntering away their lives without pleasure to themselves or advantage to the nation, withdraw from the scene, and leave their successors to tread the same idle round. In absolute monarchies the whole weight of business, civil and military, lies on the king; the children of Israel in their request for a king, urged this plea "that he may judge us, and go out before us and fight our battles." But in countries where he is neither a judge nor a general, as in England, a man would be puzzled to know what *is* his business.

The nearer any government approaches to a republic the less business there is for a king. It is somewhat difficult to find a proper name for the government of England. Sir William Meredith calls it a republic; but in its present state it is unworthy of the name, because the corrupt influence of the crown, by having all the places in its disposal, hath so effectually swallowed up the power, and eaten out the virtue of the house of commons (the republican part in the constitution) that the government of England is nearly as monarchical as that of France or Spain. Men fall out with names without understanding them. For it is the republican and not the monarchical part of the constitution of England which Englishmen glory in, viz. the liberty of choosing a house of commons from out of their own body—and it is easy to see that when republican virtue fails, slavery ensues. Why is the constitution of England sickly, but because monarchy hath poisoned the republic, the crown hath engrossed the commons?

In England a king hath little more to do than to make war and give away places; which in plain terms, is to impoverish the nation and set it together by the ears. A pretty business indeed for a man to be allowed eight hundred thousand sterling a year for, and worshipped into the bargain! Of more worth is one honest man to society and in the sight of God, than all the crowned ruffians that ever lived.

Thoughts on the Present State of American Affairs

In the following pages I offer nothing more than simple facts, plain arguments, and common sense; and have no other preliminaries to settle with the reader, than that he will divest himself of prejudice and prepossession, and suffer his reason and his feelings to determine for themselves; that he will put *on*, or rather that he will not put *off*, the true character of a man, and generously enlarge his views beyond the present day.

Volumes have been written on the subject of the struggle between England and America. Men of all ranks have embarked in the controversy, from different motives, and with various designs; but all have been ineffectual, and the period of debate is closed. Arms, as the last resource, decide the contest; the appeal was the choice of the king, and the continent hath accepted the challenge.

It hath been reported of the late Mr. Pelham (who tho' an able minister was not without his faults) that on his being attacked in the house of commons, on the score, that his measures were only of a temporary kind, replied "*they will last my time.*" Should a thought so fatal and unmanly possess the colonies in the present contest, the name of ancestors will be remembered by future generations with detestation.

The sun never shined on a cause of greater worth. 'Tis not the affair of a city, a country, a province, or a kingdom, but of a continent—of at least one eighth part of the habitable globe. 'Tis not the concern of a day, a year, or an age; posterity are virtually involved in the contest, and will be more or less affected, even to the end of time, by the proceedings now. Now is the seed time of continental union, faith and honor. The least fracture now will be like a name engraved with the point of a pin on the tender rind of a young oak; the wound will enlarge with the tree, and posterity read it in full grown characters.

By referring the matter from argument to arms, a new æra for politics is struck; a new method of thinking hath arisen. All plans, proposals, etc. prior to the nineteenth of April, *i.e.* to the commencement of hostilities, are like the almanacks of the last year; which, though proper then, are superseded and useless now. Whatever was advanced by the advocates on either side of the question then, terminated in one and the same point, viz. a union with Great-Britain; the only difference between the parties was the method of effecting it; the one proposing force, the other friendship; but it hath so far happened that the first hath failed, and the second hath withdrawn her influence.

As much hath been said of the advantages of reconciliation, which, like an agreeable dream, hath passed away and left us as we were, it is but right, that we should examine the contrary side of the argument, and inquire into some of the many material injuries which these colonies sustain, and always will sustain, by being connected with, and dependant on Great-Britain. To examine that connexion and dependance, on the principles of nature and common sense, to see what we have to trust to, if separated, and what we are to expect, if dependant.

I have heard it asserted by some, that as America hath flourished under her former connexion with Great-Britain, that the same connexion is necessary towards her future happiness, and will always have the same effect. Nothing can be more fallacious than this kind of argument. We may as well assert that because a child has thrived upon milk, that it is never to have meat, or that the first twenty years of our lives is to become a precedent for the next twenty. But even this is admitting more than is true, for I answer roundly, that America would have flourished as much, and probably much more, had no European power had any thing to do with her. The commerce, by which she hath enriched herself are the necessaries of life, and will always have a market while eating is the custom of Europe.

But she has protected us, say some. That she has engrossed us is true, and defended the continent at our expence as well as her own is admitted, and she would have defended Turkey from the same motive, viz. the sake of trade and dominion.

Alas, we have been long led away by ancient prejudices, and made large sacrifices to superstition. We have boasted the protection of Great-Britain, without considering, that her motive was *interest* not *attachment*; that she did not protect us from *our enemies* on *our account*, but from *her enemies* on *her own account*, from those who had no quarrel with us on any *other account*, and who will always be our enemies on the *same account*. Let Britain wave her pretensions to the continent, or the continent throw off the dependance, and we should be at peace with France and Spain were they at war with Britain. The miseries of Hanover last war ought to warn us against connexions.

It has lately been asserted in parliament, that the colonies have no relation to each other but through the parent country, *i.e.* that Pennsylvania and the Jerseys, and so on for the rest, are sister colonies by the way of England; this is certainly a very round-about way of proving relationship, but it is the nearest and only true way of proving enemyship, if I may so call it. France and Spain never were, nor perhaps ever will be our enemies as *Americans*, but as our being the *subjects of Great-Britain*.

But Britain is the parent country, say some. Then the more shame upon her conduct. Even brutes do not devour their young, nor savages make war upon their families; wherefore the assertion, if true, turns to her reproach; but it happens not to be true, or only partly so, and the phrase *parent* or *mother country* hath been jesuitically adopted by the king and his parasites, with a low papistical design of gaining an unfair bias on the credulous weakness of our minds. Europe, and not England, is the parent country of America. This new world hath been the asylum for the persecuted lovers of civil and religious liberty from *every part* of Europe. Hither have they fled, not from the tender embraces of the mother, but from the cruelty of the monster; and it is so far true of England, that the same tyranny which drove the first emigrants from home, pursues their descendants still.

In this extensive quarter of the globe, we forget the narrow limits of three hundred and sixty miles (the extent of England)

and carry our friendship on a larger scale; we claim brotherhood with every European christian, and triumph in the generosity of the sentiment.

It is pleasant to observe by what regular gradations we surmount the force of local prejudice, as we enlarge our acquaintance with the world. A man born in any town in England divided into parishes, will naturally associate most with his fellow parishioners (because their interests in many cases will be common) and distinguish him by the name of *neighbour*; if he meet him but a few miles from home, he drops the narrow idea of a street, and salutes him by the name of *townsman*; if he travel out of the county, and meet him in any other, he forgets the minor divisions of street and town, and calls him *countryman*, i.e. *county-man*; but if in their foreign excursions they should associate in France or any other part of *Europe*, their local remembrance would be enlarged into that of *Englishmen*. And by a just parity of reasoning, all Europeans meeting in America, or any other quarter of the globe, are *countrymen*; for England, Holland, Germany, or Sweden, when compared with the whole, stand in the same places on the larger scale, which the divisions of street, town, and county do on the smaller ones; distinctions too limited for continental minds. Not one third of the inhabitants, even of this province, are of English descent. Wherefore I reprobate the phrase of parent or mother country applied to England only, as being false, selfish, narrow and ungenerous.

But admitting, that we were all of English descent, what does it amount to? Nothing. Britain, being now an open enemy, extinguishes every other name and title: And to say that reconciliation is our duty, is truly farcical. The first king of England, of the present line (William the Conqueror) was a Frenchman, and half the Peers of England are descendants from the same country; therefore, by the same method of reasoning, England ought to be governed by France.

Much hath been said of the united strength of Britain and the colonies, that in conjunction they might bid defiance to the world. But this is mere presumption; the fate of war is uncertain, neither do the expressions mean anything; for this continent would never suffer itself to be drained of inhabitants, to support the British arms in either Asia, Africa, or Europe.

Besides what have we to do with setting the world at defiance? Our plan is commerce, and that, well attended to, will secure us the peace and friendship of all Europe; because, it is the interest of all Europe to have America a *free port*. Her trade will always be a protection, and her barrenness of gold and silver secure her from invaders.

I challenge the warmest advocate for reconciliation, to shew, a single advantage that this continent can reap, by being connected with Great Britain. I repeat the challenge, not a single advantage is derived. Our corn will fetch its price in any market in Europe, and our imported goods must be paid for buy them where we will.

But the injuries and disadvantages we sustain by that connection, are without number; and our duty to mankind at large, as well as to ourselves, instruct us to renounce the alliance: Because, any submission to, or dependance on Great-Britain, tends directly to involve this continent in European wars and quarrels; and sets us at variance with nations, who would otherwise seek our friendship, and against whom, we have neither anger nor complaint. As Europe is our market for trade, we ought to form no partial connection with any part of it. It is the true interest of America to steer clear of European contentions, which she never can do, while by her dependence on Britain, she is made the make-weight in the scale of British politics.

Europe is too thickly planted with kingdoms to be long at peace, and whenever a war breaks out between England and any foreign power, the trade of America goes to ruin, *because of her connection with Britain*. The next war may not turn out like the last, and should it not, the advocates for reconciliation now will be wishing for separation then, because, neutrality in that case, would be a safer convoy than a man of war. Everything that is right or natural pleads for separation. The blood of the slain, the weeping voice of nature cries, 'TIS TIME TO PART. Even the distance at which the Almighty hath placed England and America, is a strong and natural proof, that the authority of the one, over the other, was never the design of Heaven. The time likewise at which the continent was discovered, adds weight to the argument, and the manner in which it was peopled encreases the force of it. The reformation was preceded by the discovery of America, as if the Almighty graciously meant to open a sanctuary to the persecuted in future years, when home should afford neither friendship nor safety.

The authority of Great-Britain over this continent, is a form of government, which sooner or later must have an end: And a serious mind can draw no true pleasure by looking forward, under the painful and positive conviction, that what he calls "the present constitution" is merely temporary. As parents, we can have no joy, knowing that *this government* is not sufficiently lasting to ensure anything which we may bequeath to posterity: And by a plain method of argument, as we are running the next generation into debt, we ought to do the work of it, otherwise we use them meanly and pitifully. In order to discover the line of our duty rightly, we should take our children in our hand, and fix our station a few years farther into life; that eminence will present a prospect, which a few present fears and prejudices conceal from our sight.

Though I would carefully avoid giving unnecessary offence, yet I am inclined to believe, that all those who espouse the doctrine of reconciliation, may be included within the following descriptions. Interested men, who are not to be trusted; weak men, who *cannot* see; prejudiced men, who *will not* see; and a certain set of moderate men, who think better of the European world than it deserves; and this last class, by an ill-judged deliberation, will be the cause of more calamities to this continent, than all the other three.

It is the good fortune of many to live distant from the scene of sorrow; the evil is not sufficient brought to *their* doors to make *them* feel the precariousness with which all American property is possessed. But let our imaginations transport us for a few moments to Boston, that seat of wretchedness will teach us wisdom, and instruct us forever to renounce a power in whom we can have no trust. The inhabitants of that unfortunate city, who but a few months ago were in ease and affluence, have now, no other alternative than to stay and starve, or turn out to beg. Endangered by the fire of their friends if they continue within the city, and plundered by the soldiery if they leave it. In their present condition they are prisoners without the hope of redemption, and in a general attack for their relief, they would be exposed to the fury of both armies.

Men of passive tempers look somewhat lightly over the offences of Britain, and, still hoping for the best, are apt to call out, "*Come, come, we shall be friends again, for all this.*" But examine the passions and feelings of mankind, Bring the doctrine of reconciliation to the touchstone of nature, and then tell me, whether you can hereafter love, honour, and faithfully serve the power that hath carried fire and sword into your land? If you cannot do all these, then are you only deceiving yourselves, and by your delay bringing ruin upon posterity. Your future connection with Britain, whom you can neither love nor honour, will be forced and unnatural, and being formed only on the plan of present convenience, will in a little time fall into a relapse more wretched than the first. But if you say, you can still pass the violations over, then I ask, Hath your house been burnt? Hath your property been destroyed before your face? Are your wife and children destitute of a bed to lie on, or bread to live on? Have you lost a parent or a child by their hands, and yourself the ruined and wretched survivor? If you have not, then are you not a judge of those who have. But if you have, and still can shake hands with the murderers, then are you unworthy of the name of husband, father, friend, or lover, and whatever may be your rank or title in life, you have the heart of a coward, and the spirit of a sycophant.

This is not inflaming or exaggerating matters, but trying them by those feelings and affections which nature justifies, and without which, we should be incapable of discharging the social duties of life, or enjoying the felicities of it. I mean not to exhibit horror for the purpose of provoking revenge, but to awaken us from fatal and unmanly slumbers, that we may pursue determinately some fixed object. It is not in the power of Britain or of Europe to conquer America, if she do not conquer herself by *delay* and *timidity*. The present winter is worth an age if rightly employed, but if lost or neglected, the whole continent will partake of the misfortune; and there is no punishment which that man will not deserve, be he who, or what, or where he will, that may be the means of sacrificing a season so precious and useful.

It is repugnant to reason, to the universal order of things to all examples from former ages, to suppose, that this continent can longer remain subject to any external power. The most sanguine in Britain does not think so. The utmost stretch of human wisdom cannot, at this time, compass a plan short of separation, which can promise the continent even a year's security. Reconciliation is *now* a fallacious dream. Nature hath deserted the connexion, and Art cannot supply her place. For, as Milton wisely expresses, "never can true reconcilement grow where wounds of deadly hate have pierced so deep."

Every quiet method for peace hath been ineffectual. Our prayers have been rejected with disdain; and only tended to convince us, that nothing flatters vanity, or confirms obstinacy in Kings more than repeated petitioning—and nothing hath contributed more than that very measure to make the Kings of Europe absolute: Witness Denmark and Sweden. Wherefore, since nothing but blows will do, for God's sake, let us come to a final separation, and not leave the next generation to be cutting throats, under the violated unmeaning names of parent and child.

To say, they will never attempt it again is idle and visionary, we thought so at the repeal of the stamp-act, yet a year or two undeceived us; as well may we suppose that nations, which have been once defeated, will never renew the quarrel.

As to government matters, it is not in the power of Britain to do this continent justice: The business of it will soon be too weighty, and intricate, to be managed with any tolerable degree of convenience, by a power, so distant from us, and so very ignorant of us; for if they cannot conquer us, they cannot govern us. To be always running three or four thousand miles with a tale or a petition, waiting four or five months for an answer, which when obtained requires five or six more to explain it in, will in a few years be looked upon as folly and childishness—There was a time when it was proper, and there is a proper time for it to cease.

Small islands not capable of protecting themselves, are the proper objects for kingdoms to take under their care; but there is something very absurd, in supposing a continent to be perpetually governed by an island. In no instance hath nature made the satellite larger than its primary planet, and as England and America, with respect to each other, reverses the common order of nature, it is evident they belong to different systems: England to Europe, America to itself.

I am not induced by motives of pride, party, or resentment to espouse the doctrine of separation and independance; I am clearly, positively, and conscientiously persuaded that it is the true interest of this continent to be so; that everything short of *that* is mere patchwork, that it can afford no lasting felicity,— that it is leaving the sword to our children, and shrinking back at a time, when, a little more, a little farther, would have rendered this continent the glory of the earth.

As Britain hath not manifested the least inclination towards a compromise, we may be assured that no terms can be obtained worthy the acceptance of the continent, or anyways equal to the expence of blood and treasure we have been already put to.

The object, contended for, ought always to bear some just proportion to the expence. The removal of North, or the whole detestable junto, is a matter unworthy the millions we have expended. A temporary stoppage of trade, was an inconvenience, which would have sufficiently ballanced the repeal of all the acts complained of, had such repeals been obtained; but if the whole continent must take up arms, if every man must be a soldier, it is scarcely worth our while to fight against a contemptible ministry only. Dearly, dearly, do we pay for the repeal of the acts, if that is all we fight for; for in a just estimation, it is as great a folly to pay a Bunker-hill price for law, as for land. As I have always considered the independancy of this continent, as an event, which sooner or later must arrive, so from the late rapid progress of the continent to maturity, the event could not be far off. Wherefore, on the breaking out of hostilities, it was not worth the while to have disputed a matter, which time would have finally redressed, unless we meant to be in earnest; otherwise, it is like wasting an estate on a suit at law, to regulate the trespasses of a tenant, whose lease is just expiring. No man was a warmer wisher for reconciliation than myself, before the fatal nineteenth of April 1775, but the moment the event of that day was made known, I rejected the hardened, sullen tempered Pharaoh of England forever; and disdain the wretch, that with the pretended title of FATHER OF HIS PEOPLE can unfeelingly hear of their slaughter, and composedly sleep with their blood upon his soul.

But admitting that matters were now made up, what would be the event? I answer, the ruin of the continent. And that for several reasons.

First. The powers of governing still remaining in the hands of the king, he will have a negative over the whole legislation of this continent. And as he hath shewn himself such an inveterate enemy to liberty, and discovered such a thirst for arbitrary power; is he, or is he not, a proper man to say to these colonies, "*You shall make no laws but what I please.*" And is there any inhabitant in America so ignorant, as not to know, that according to what is called the *present constitution*, that this continent can make no laws but what the king gives leave to; and is there any man so unwise, as not to see, that (considering what has happened) he will suffer no law to be made here, but such as suit *his* purpose. We may be as effectually enslaved by the want of laws in America, as by submitting to laws made for us in England. After matters are made up (as it is called) can there be any doubt, but the whole power of the crown will be exerted, to keep this continent as low and humble as possible? Instead of going forward we shall go backward, or be perpetually quarrelling or ridiculously petitioning.—We are already greater than the king wishes us to be, and will he not hereafter endeavour to make us less? To bring the matter to one point. Is the power who is jealous of our prosperity, a proper power to govern us? Whoever says *No* to this question is an *independant*, for independency means no more, than, whether we shall make our own laws, or whether the king, the greatest enemy this continent hath, or can have, shall tell us "*there shall be no laws but such as I like.*"

But the king you will say has a negative in England; the people there can make no laws without his consent. In point of right and good order, there is something very ridiculous, that a youth of twenty-one (which hath often happened) shall say to several millions of people, older and wiser than himself, I forbid this or that act of yours to be law. But in this place I decline this sort of reply, though I will never cease to expose the absurdity of it, and only answer, that England being the King's residence, and America not so, makes quite another case. The king's negative *here* is ten times more dangerous and fatal than it can be in England, for *there* he will scarcely refuse his consent to a bill for putting England into as strong a state of defence as possible, and in America he would never suffer such a bill to be passed.

America is only a secondary object in the system of British politics, England consults the good of *this* country, no farther than it answers her *own* purpose. Wherefore, her own interest leads her to suppress the growth of *ours* in every case which doth not promote her advantage, or in the least interferes with it. A pretty state we should soon be in under such a second-hand government, considering what has happened! Men do not change from enemies to friends by the alteration of a name: And in order to shew that reconciliation *now* is a dangerous doctrine, I affirm, *that it would be policy in the king at this time, to repeal the acts for the sake of reinstating himself in the government of the provinces;* in order, that *he may accomplish by craft and subtilty, in the long run, what he cannot do by force and violence in the short one.* Reconciliation and ruin are nearly related.

Secondly. That as even the best terms, which we can expect to obtain, can amount to no more than a temporary expedient, or a kind of government by guardianship, which can last no longer than till the colonies come of age, so the general face and state of things, in the interim, will be unsettled and unpromising. Emigrants of property will not choose to come to a country whose form of government hangs but by a thread, and who is everyday tottering on the brink of commotion and disturbance; and numbers of the present inhabitants would lay hold of the interval, to dispense of their effects, and quit the continent.

But the most powerful of all arguments, is, that nothing but independance, i.e. a continental form of government, can keep the peace of the continent and preserve it inviolate from civil wars. I dread the event of a reconciliation with Britain now, as it is more than probable, that it will be followed by a revolt somewhere or other, the consequences of which may be far more fatal than all the malice of Britain.

Thousands are already ruined by British barbarity; (thousands more will probably suffer the same fate) Those men have other feelings than us who have nothing suffered. All they *now* possess is liberty, what they before enjoyed is sacrificed to its service, and having nothing more to lose, they disdain submission. Besides, the general temper of the colonies, towards a British government, will be like that of a youth, who is nearly out of his time; they will care very little about her. And a government which cannot preserve the peace, is no government at all, and in that case we pay our money for nothing; and pray what is it that Britain can do, whose power will be wholly on paper, should a civil tumult break out the very day after reconciliation? I have heard some men say, many of whom I believe spoke without thinking, that they dreaded an independance, fearing that it would produce civil wars. It is but seldom that our first thoughts are truly correct, and that is the case here; for there are ten times more to dread from a patched up connexion than from independance. I make the sufferers case my own, and I protest, that were I driven from house and home, my property destroyed, and my circumstances ruined, that as man, sensible of injuries, I could never relish the doctrine of reconciliation, or consider myself bound thereby.

The colonies have manifested such a spirit of good order and obedience to continental government, as is sufficient to make every reasonable person easy and happy on that head. No man can assign the least pretence for his fears, on any other grounds, than such as are truly childish and ridiculous, viz. that one colony will be striving for superiority over another.

Where there are no distinctions there can be no superiority, perfect equality affords no temptation. The republics of Europe are all (and we may say always) in peace. Holland and Swisserland are without wars, foreign or domestic: Monarchical governments, it is true, are never long at rest; the crown itself is a temptation to enterprizing ruffians at *home*; and that degree of pride and insolence ever attendant on regal authority, swells into a rupture with foreign powers, in instances, where a republican government, by being formed on more natural principles, would negociate the mistake.

If there is any true cause of fear respecting independance, it is because no plan is yet laid down. Men do not see their way out—Wherefore, as an opening into that business, I offer the following hints; at the same time modestly affirming, that I have no other opinion of them myself, than that they may be the means of giving rise to something better. Could the straggling thoughts of individuals be collected, they would frequently form materials for wise and able men to improve into useful matter.

Let the assemblies be annual, with a President only. The representation more equal. Their business wholly domestic, and subject to the authority of a Continental Congress.

Let each colony be divided into six, eight, or ten, convenient districts, each district to send a proper number of delegates to Congress, so that each colony send at least thirty. The whole number in Congress will be at least 390. Each Congress to sit and to choose a president by the following method. When the delegates are met, let a colony be taken from the whole thirteen colonies by lot, after which, let the whole Congress choose (by ballot) a president from out of the delegates of *that* province. In the next Congress, let a colony be taken by lot from twelve only, omitting that colony from which the president was taken in the former Congress, and so proceeding on till the whole thirteen shall have had their proper rotation. And in order that nothing may pass into a law but what is satisfactorily just, not less than three fifths of the Congress to be called a majority.—He that will promote discord, under a government so equally formed as this, would have joined Lucifer in his revolt.

But as there is a peculiar delicacy, from whom, or in what manner, this business must first arise, and as it seems most agreeable and consistent that it should come from some intermediate body between the governed and the governors, that is, between the Congress and the people, let a *Continental Conference* be held, in the following manner, and for the following purpose.

A committee of twenty-six members of Congress, viz. two for each colony. Two members from each House of Assembly, or Provincial Convention; and five representatives of the people at large, to be chosen in the capital city or town of each province, for, and in behalf of the whole province, by as many qualified voters as shall think proper to attend from all parts of the province for that purpose; or, if more convenient, the representatives may be chosen in two or three of the most populous parts thereof. In this conference, thus assembled, will be united, the two grand principles of business, *knowledge* and *power*. The members of Congress, Assemblies, or Conventions, by having had experience in national concerns, will be able and useful counsellors, and the whole, being impowered by the people, will have a truly legal authority.

The conferring members being met, let their business be to frame a *Continental Charter*, or Charter of the United Colonies; (answering to what is called the Magna Charta of England) fixing the number and manner of choosing members of Congress, members of Assembly, with their date of sitting, and drawing the line of business and jurisdiction between them: (Always remembering, that our strength is continental, not provincial:) Securing freedom and property to all men, and above all things, the free exercise of religion, according to the dictates of conscience; with such other matter as is necessary for a charter to contain. Immediately after which, the said Conference to dissolve, and the bodies which shall be chosen comfortable to the said charter, to be the legislators and governors of this continent for the time being: Whose peace and happiness, may God preserve, Amen.

Should anybody of men be hereafter delegated for this or some similar purpose, I offer them the following extracts from that wise observer on governments *Dragonetti*. "The science" says he "of the politician consists in fixing the true point of happiness and freedom. Those men would deserve the gratitude of ages, who should discover a mode of government that contained the greatest sum of individual happiness, with the least national expense.

Dragonetti on virtue and rewards."

But where says some is the King of America? I'll tell you Friend, he reigns above, and doth not make havoc of mankind like the Royal Brute of Britain. Yet that we may not appear to be defective even in earthly honors, let a day be solemnly set apart for proclaiming the charter; let it be brought forth placed on the divine law, the word of God; let a crown be placed thereon, by which the world may know, that so far as we approve of monarchy, that in America THE LAW IS KING. For as in absolute governments the King is law, so in free countries the law *ought* to be King; and there ought to be no other. But lest any ill use should afterwards arise, let the crown at the conclusion of the ceremony be demolished, and scattered among the people whose right it is.

A government of our own is our natural right: And when a man seriously reflects on the precariousness of human affairs, he will become convinced, that it is infinitely wiser and safer, to form a constitution of our own in a cool deliberate manner, while we have it in our power, than to trust such an interesting event to time and chance. If we omit it now, some Massanello[1] may hereafter arise, who laying hold of popular disquietudes, may collect together the desperate and the discontented, and by assuming to themselves the powers of government, may sweep away the liberties of the continent like a deluge. Should the government of America return again into the hands of Britain, the tottering situation of things, will be a temptation for some desperate adventurer to try his fortune; and in such a case, what relief can Britain give? Ere she could hear the news, the fatal business might be done; and ourselves suffering like the wretched Britons under the oppression of the Conqueror. Ye that oppose independance now, ye know not what ye do; ye are opening a door to eternal tyranny, by keeping vacant the seat of government. There are thousands, and tens of thousands, who would think it glorious to expel from the continent, that barbarous and hellish

---

1. Thomas Anello, otherwise Massanello, a fisherman of Naples, who after spiriting up his countrymen in the public market place, against the oppressions of the Spaniards, to whom the place was then subject, prompted them to revolt, and in the space of a day became king.

power, which hath stirred up the Indians and Negroes to destroy us, the cruelty hath a double guilt, it is dealing brutally by us, and treacherously by them.

To talk of friendship with those in whom our reason forbids us to have faith, and our affections wounded through a thousand pores instruct us to detest, is madness and folly. Everyday wears out the little remains of kindred between us and them, and can there be any reason to hope, that as the relationship expires, the affection will increase, or that we shall agree better, when we have ten times more and greater concerns to quarrel over than ever?

Ye that tell us of harmony and reconciliation, can ye restore to us the time that is past? Can ye give to prostitution its former innocence? Neither can ye reconcile Britain and America. The last cord now is broken, the people of England are presenting addresses against us. There are injuries which nature cannot forgive; she would cease to be nature if she did. As well can the lover forgive the ravisher of his mistress, as the continent forgive the murders of Britain. The Almighty hath implanted in us these unextinguishable feelings for good and wise purposes. They are the guardians of his image in our hearts. They distinguish us from the herd of common animals. The social compact would dissolve, and justice be extirpated the earth, or have only a casual existence were we callous to the touches of affection. The robber, and the murderer, would often escape unpunished, did not the injuries which our tempers sustain, provoke us into justice.

O ye that love mankind! Ye that dare oppose, not only the tyranny, but the tyrant, stand forth! Every spot of the old world is overrun with oppression. Freedom hath been hunted round the globe. Asia, and Africa, have long expelled her—Europe regards her like a stranger, and England hath given her warning to depart. O! receive the fugitive, and prepare in time an asylum for mankind.

Of the Present Ability of America, with Some Miscellaneous Reflexions

I HAVE NEVER MET WITH a man, either in England or America, who hath not confessed his opinion, that a separation between the countries, would take place one time or other: And there is no instance, in which we have shewn less judgment, than in endeavouring to describe, what we call, the ripeness or fitness of the Continent for independance.

As all men allow the measure, and vary only in their opinion of the time, let us, in order to remove mistakes, take a general survey of things, and endeavour, if possible, to find out the *very* time. But we need not go far, the inquiry ceases at once, for, the *time hath found us*. The general concurrence, the glorious union of all things prove the fact.

It is not in numbers, but in unity, that our great strength lies; yet our present numbers are sufficient to repel the force of all the world. The Continent hath, at this time, the largest body of armed and disciplined men of any power under Heaven; and is just arrived at that pitch of strength, in which no single colony is able to support itself, and the whole, when united, can accomplish the matter, and either more, or, less than this, might be fatal in its effects. Our land force is already sufficient, and as to naval affairs, we cannot be insensible, that Britain would never suffer an American man of war to be built, while the continent remained in her hands. Wherefore, we should be no forwarder an hundred years hence in that branch, than we are now; but the truth is, we should be less so, because the timber of the country is everyday diminishing, and that, which will remain at last, will be far off and difficult to procure.

Were the continent crowded with inhabitants, her sufferings under the present circumstances would be intolerable. The more sea port towns we had, the more should we have both to defend and to lose. Our present numbers are so happily proportioned to our wants, that no man need be idle. The diminution of trade affords an army, and the necessities of an army create a new trade.

Debts we have none; and whatever we may contract on this account will serve as a glorious memento of our virtue. Can we but leave posterity with a settled form of government, an independant constitution of its own, the purchase at any price will be cheap. But to expend millions for the sake of getting a few vile acts repealed, and routing the present ministry only, is unworthy the charge, and is using posterity with the utmost cruelty; because it is leaving them the great work to do, and a debt upon their backs, from which they derive no advantage. Such a thought is unworthy a man of honor, and is the true characteristic of a narrow heart and a pedling politician.

The debt we may contract doth not deserve our regard if the work be but accomplished. No nation ought to be without a debt. A national debt is a national bond; and when it bears no interest, is in no case a grievance. Britain is oppressed with a debt of upwards of one hundred and forty millions sterling, for which she pays upwards of four millions interest. And as a compensation for her debt, she has a large navy; America is without a debt, and without a navy; yet for the twentieth part of the English national debt, could have a navy as large again. The navy of England is not worth, at this time, more than three millions and an half sterling.

The first and second editions of this pamphlet were published without the following calculations, which are now given as a proof that the above estimation of the navy is just. *See Entic's naval history, intro.* page 56.

The charge of building a ship of each rate, and furnishing her with masts, yards, sails and rigging, together with a proportion of eight months boatswain's and carpenter's sea-stores, as calculated by Mr. Burchett, Secretary to the navy.

		£ (pounds sterling)
For a ship of 100 guns	=	35,553
90	=	29,886
80	=	23,638
70	=	17,785
60	=	14,197
50	=	10,606
40	=	7,558
30	=	5,846
20	=	3,710

And from hence it is easy to sum up the value, or cost rather, of the whole British navy, which in the year 1757, when it was at its greatest glory consisted of the following ships and guns:

Ships.	Guns.	Cost of one.	Cost of all.
		Cost in £	
6	100	35,553	213,318
12	90	29,886	358,632
12	80	23,638	283,656
43	70	17,785	764,755
35	60	14,197	496,895
40	50	10,606	424,240
45	40	7,558	340,110
58	20	3,710	215,180
85	Sloops, bombs and fireships, one with another, at	2,000	170,000
Cost			3,266,786
Remains for Guns			233,214
			3,500,000

No country on the globe is so happily situated, or so internally capable of raising a fleet as America. Tar, timber, iron, and cordage are her natural produce. We need go abroad for nothing. Whereas the Dutch, who make large profits by hiring out their ships of war to the Spaniards and Portuguese, are obliged to import most of the materials they use. We ought to view the building a fleet as an article of commerce, it being the natural manufactory of this country. It is the best money we can lay out. A navy when finished is worth more than it cost. And is that nice point in national policy, in which commerce and protection are united. Let us build; if we want them not, we can sell; and by that means replace our paper currency with ready gold and silver.

In point of manning a fleet, people in general run into great errors; it is not necessary that one fourth part should be sailors. The Terrible privateer, Captain Death, stood the hottest engagement of any ship last war, yet had not twenty sailors on board, though her complement of men was upwards of two hundred. A few able and social sailors will soon instruct a sufficient number of active landmen in the common work of a ship. Wherefore, we never can be more capable to begin on maritime matters than now, while our timber is standing, our fisheries blocked up, and our sailors and shipwrights out of employ. Men of war, of seventy and eighty guns were built forty years ago in New-England, and why not the same now? Ship-building is America's greatest pride, and in which, she will in time excel the whole world. The great empires of the east are mostly inland, and consequently excluded from the possibility of rivalling her. Africa is in a state of barbarism; and no power in Europe, hath either such an extent of coast, or such an internal supply of materials. Where nature hath given the one, she has withheld the other; to America only hath she been liberal of both. The vast empire of Russia is almost shut out from the sea; wherefore, her boundless forests, her tar, iron, and cordage are only articles of commerce.

In point of safety, ought we to be without a fleet? We are not the little people now, which we were sixty years ago; at that time we might have trusted our property in the streets, or fields rather; and slept securely without locks or bolts to our doors or windows. The case now is altered, and our methods of defence, ought to improve with our increase of property. A common pirate, twelve months ago, might have come up the Delaware, and laid the city of Philadelphia under instant contribution, for what sum he pleased; and the same might have happened to other places. Nay, any daring fellow, in a brig of fourteen or sixteen guns, might have robbed the whole Continent, and carried off half a million of money. These are circumstances which demand our attention, and point out the necessity of naval protection.

Some, perhaps, will say, that after we have made it up with Britain, she will protect us. Can we be so unwise as to mean, that she shall keep a navy in our harbours for that purpose? Common sense will tell us, that the power which hath endeavoured to subdue us, is of all others, the most improper to defend us. Conquest may be effected under the pretence of friendship; and ourselves, after a long and brave resistance, be at last cheated into slavery. And if her ships are not to be admitted into our harbours, I would ask, how is she to protect us? A navy three or four thousand miles off can be of little use, and on sudden emergencies, none at all. Wherefore, if we must hereafter protect ourselves, why not do it for ourselves? Why do it for another?

The English list of ships of war, is long and formidable, but not a tenth part of them are at any one time fit for service, numbers of them not in being; yet their names are pompously continued in the list, if only a plank be left of the ship: and not a fifth part, of such as are fit for service, can be spared on anyone station at one time. The East and West Indies, Mediterranean, Africa, and other parts over which Britain extends her claim, make large demands upon her navy. From a mixture of prejudice and inattention, we have contracted a false notion respecting the navy of England, and have talked as if we should have the whole of it to encounter at once, and for that reason, supposed, that we must have one as large; which not being instantly practicable, have been made use of by a set of disguised Tories to discourage our beginning thereon. Nothing can be farther from truth than this; for if America had only a twentieth part of the naval force of Britain, she would be by far an over match for her; because, as we neither have, nor claim any foreign dominion, our whole force would be employed on our own coast, where we should, in the long run, have two to one the advantage of those who had three or four thousand miles to sail over, before they could attack us, and the same distance to return in order to refit and recruit. And although Britain by her fleet, hath a check over our trade to Europe, we have as large a one over her trade to the West-Indies, which, by laying in the neighbourhood of the Continent, is entirely at its mercy.

Some method might be fallen on to keep up a naval force in time of peace, if we should not judge it necessary to support a constant navy. If premiums were to be given to merchants, to build and employ in their service ships mounted with twenty, thirty, forty or fifty guns, (the premiums to be in proportion to the loss of bulk to the merchants) fifty or sixty of those ships, with a few guardships on constant duty, would keep up a sufficient navy, and that without burdening ourselves with the evil so loudly complained of in England, of suffering their fleet, in time of peace to lie rotting in the docks. To unite the sinews of commerce and defense is sound policy; for when our strength and our riches play into each other's hand, we need fear no external enemy.

In almost every article of defense we abound. Hemp flourishes even to rankness, so that we need not want cordage. Our iron is superior to that of other countries. Our small arms equal to any in the world. Cannon we can cast at pleasure. Saltpetre and gunpowder we are everyday producing. Our knowledge is hourly improving. Resolution is our inherent character, and courage hath never yet forsaken us. Wherefore, what is it that we want? Why is it that we hesitate? From Britain we can expect nothing but ruin. If she is once admitted to the government of America again, this Continent will not be worth living in. Jealousies will be always arising; insurrections will be constantly happening; and who will go forth to quell them? Who will venture his life to reduce his own countrymen to a foreign obedience? The difference between Pennsylvania and Connecticut, respecting some unlocated lands, shews the insignificance of a British government, and fully proves, that nothing but Continental authority can regulate Continental matters.

Another reason why the present time is preferable to all others, is, that the fewer our numbers are, the more land there is yet unoccupied, which instead of being lavished by the king on his worthless dependants, may be hereafter applied, not only to the discharge of the present debt, but to the constant support of government. No nation under heaven hath such an advantage as this.

The infant state of the Colonies, as it is called, so far from being against, is an argument in favour of independence. We are sufficiently numerous, and were we more so, we might be less united. It is a matter worthy of observation, that the more a country is peopled, the smaller their armies are. In military numbers, the ancients far exceeded the moderns: and the reason is evident. For trade being the consequence of population, men become too much absorbed thereby to attend to anything else. Commerce diminishes the spirit, both of patriotism and military defence. And history sufficiently informs us, that the bravest achievements were always accomplished in the non-age of a nation. With the increase of commerce, England hath lost its spirit. The city of London, notwithstanding its numbers, submits to continued insults with the patience of a coward. The more men have to lose, the less willing are they to venture. The rich are in general slaves to fear, and submit to courtly power with the trembling duplicity of a Spaniel.

Youth is the seed time of good habits, as well in nations as in individuals. It might be difficult, if not impossible, to form the Continent into one government half a century hence. The vast variety of interests, occasioned by an increase of trade and population, would create confusion. Colony would be against colony. Each being able might scorn each other's assistance: and while the proud and foolish gloried in their little distinctions, the wise would lament, that the union had not been formed before. Wherefore, the *present time* is the *true time* for establishing it. The intimacy which is contracted in infancy, and the friendship which is formed in misfortune, are, of all others, the most lasting and unalterable. Our present union is marked with both these characters: we are young and we have been distressed; but our concord hath withstood our troubles, and fixes a memorable area for posterity to glory in.

The present time, likewise, is that peculiar time, which never happens to a nation but once, viz. the time of forming itself into a government. Most nations have let slip the opportunity, and by that means have been compelled to receive laws from their conquerors, instead of making laws for themselves. First, they had a king, and then a form of government; whereas, the articles or charter of government, should be formed first, and men delegated to execute them afterward: but from the errors of other nations, let us learn wisdom, and lay hold of the present opportunity—*To begin government at the right end*.

When William the Conqueror subdued England, he gave them law at the point of the sword; and until we consent, that the seat of government, in America, be legally and authoritatively occupied, we shall be in danger of having it filled by some fortunate ruffian, who may treat us in the same manner, and then, where will be our freedom? where our property?

As to religion, I hold it to be the indispensable duty of all government, to protect all conscientious professors thereof, and I know of no other business which government hath to do therewith. Let a man throw aside that narrowness of soul, that selfishness of principle, which the niggards of all professions are so unwilling to part with, and he will be at once delivered of his fears on that head. Suspicion is the companion of mean souls, and the bane of all good society. For myself, I fully and conscientiously believe, that it is the will of the Almighty, that there should be diversity of religious opinions among us: It affords a larger field for our Christian kindness. Were we all of one way of thinking, our religious dispositions would want matter for probation; and on this liberal principle, I look on the various denominations among us, to be like children of the same family, differing only, in what is called, their Christian names.

In page forty, I threw out a few thoughts on the propriety of a Continental Charter, (for I only presume to offer hints, not plans) and in this place, I take the liberty of re-mentioning the subject, by observing, that a charter is to be understood as a bond of solemn obligation, which the whole enters into, to support the right of every separate part, whether of religion, personal freedom, or property. A firm bargain and a right reckoning make long friends.

In a former page I likewise mentioned the necessity of a large and equal representation; and there is no political matter which more deserves our attention. A small number of electors, or a small number of representatives, are equally dangerous. But if the number of the representatives be not only small, but unequal, the danger is increased. As an instance of this, I mention the following; when the Associators petition was before the House of Assembly of Pennsylvania; twenty-eight members only were present, all the Bucks county members, being eight, voted against it, and had seven of the Chester members done the same, this whole province had been governed by two counties only, and this danger it is always exposed to. The unwarrantable stretch likewise, which that house made in their last sitting, to gain an undue authority over the delegates of that province, ought to warn the people at large, how they trust power out of their own hands. A set of instructions for the Delegates were put together, which in point of sense and business would have dishonoured a schoolboy, and after being approved by a *few*, a *very few* without doors, were carried into the House, and there passed *in behalf of the whole colony*; whereas, did the whole colony know, with what ill-will that House hath entered on some necessary public measures, they would not hesitate a moment to think them unworthy of such a trust.

Immediate necessity makes many things convenient, which if continued would grow into oppressions. Expedience and right are different things. When the calamities of America required a consultation, there was no method so ready, or at that time so proper, as to appoint persons from the several Houses of Assembly for that purpose; and the wisdom with which they have proceeded hath preserved this continent from ruin. But as it is more than probable that we shall never be without a CONGRESS, every well wisher to good order, must own, that the mode for choosing members of that body, deserves consideration. And I put it as a question to those, who make a study of mankind, whether *representation and election* is not too great a power for one and the same body of men to possess? When we are planning for posterity, we ought to remember, that virtue is not hereditary.

It is from our enemies that we often gain excellent maxims, and are frequently surprised into reason by their mistakes. Mr. Cornwall (one of the Lords of the Treasury) treated the petition of the New-York Assembly with contempt, because *that* House, he said, consisted but of twenty-six members, which trifling number, he argued, could not with decency be put for the whole. We thank him for his involuntary honesty.[2]

To conclude, however strange it may appear to some, or however unwilling they may be to think so, matters not, but many strong and striking reasons may be given, to shew, that nothing can settle our affairs so expeditiously as an open and determined declaration for independance. Some of which are,

First.—It is the custom of nations, when any two are at war, for some other powers, not engaged in the quarrel, to step in as mediators, and bring about the preliminaries of a peace: but while America calls herself the Subject of Great-Britain, no power, however well disposed she may be, can offer her mediation. Wherefore, in our present state we may quarrel on forever.

Secondly.—It is unreasonable to suppose, that France or Spain will give us any kind of assistance, if we mean only, to make use of that assistance for the purpose of repairing the breach, and strengthening the connection between Britain and America; because, those powers would be sufferers by the consequences.

Thirdly.—While we profess ourselves the subjects of Britain, we must, in the eye of foreign nations, be considered as rebels. The precedent is somewhat dangerous to *their peace*, for men to be in arms under the name of subjects; we, on the spot, can solve the paradox: but to unite resistance and subjection, requires an idea much too refined for common understanding.

Fourthly.—Were a manifesto to be published, and despatched to foreign courts, setting forth the miseries we have endured, and the peaceable methods we have ineffectually used for redress; declaring, at the same time, that not being able, any longer, to live happily or safely under the cruel disposition of the British court, we had been driven to the necessity of breaking off all connections with her; at the same time, assuring all such courts of our peaceable disposition towards them, and of our desire of entering into trade with them: Such a memorial would produce

---

2. Those who would fully understand of what great consequence a large and equal representation is to a state, should read Burgh's political disquisitions.

more good effects to this Continent, than if a ship were freighted with petitions to Britain.

Under our present denomination of British subjects, we can neither be received nor heard abroad: The custom of all courts is against us, and will be so, until, by an independance, we take rank with other nations.

These proceedings may at first appear strange and difficult; but, like all other steps which we have already passed over, will in a little time become familiar and agreeable; and, until an independance is declared, the Continent will feel itself like a man who continues putting off some unpleasant business from day today, yet knows it must be done, hates to set about it, wishes it over, and is continually haunted with the thoughts of its necessity.

Appendix

SINCE THE PUBLICATION OF THE first edition of this pamphlet, or rather, on the same day on which it came out, the King's Speech made its appearance in this city. Had the spirit of prophecy directed the birth of this production, it could not have brought it forth, at a more seasonable juncture, or a more necessary time. The bloody mindedness of the one, shew the necessity of pursuing the doctrine of the other. Men read by way of revenge. And the Speech, instead of terrifying, prepared a way for the manly principles of Independance.

Ceremony, and even, silence, from whatever motive they may arise, have a hurtful tendency, when they give the least degree of countenance to base and wicked performances; wherefore, if this maxim be admitted, it naturally follows, that the King's Speech, as being a piece of finished villainy, deserved, and still deserves, a general execration both by the Congress and the people. Yet, as the domestic tranquillity of a nation, depends greatly, on the *chastity* of what may properly be called *national manners*, it is often better, to pass somethings over in silent disdain, than to make use of such new methods of dislike, as might introduce the least innovation, on that guardian of our peace and safety. And, perhaps, it is chiefly owing to this prudent delicacy, that the

King's Speech, hath not, before now, suffered a public execution. The Speech if it may be called one, is nothing better than a wilful audacious libel against the truth, the common good, and the existence of mankind; and is a formal and pompous method of offering up human sacrifices to the pride of tyrants. But this general massacre of mankind, is one of the privileges, and the certain consequence of Kings; for as nature knows them *not*, they know *not her*, and although they are beings of our *own* creating, they know not *us*, and are become the gods of their creators. The Speech hath one good quality, which is, that it is not calculated to deceive, neither can we, even if we would, be deceived by it. Brutality and tyranny appear on the face of it. It leaves us at no loss: And every line convinces, even in the moment of reading, that He, who hunts the woods for prey, the naked and untutored Indian, is less a Savage than the King of Britain.

Sir John Dalrymple, the putative father of a whining jesuitical piece, fallaciously called, "*The Address of the people of England to the inhabitants of America*," hath, perhaps, from a vain supposition, that the people *here* were to be frightened at the pomp and description of a king, given, (though very unwisely on his part) the real character of the present one: "But" says this writer, "if you are inclined to pay compliments to an administration, which we do not complain of," (meaning the Marquis of Rockingham's at the repeal of the Stamp Act) "it is very unfair in you to withhold them from that prince, *by whose nod alone they were permitted to do anything*." This is toryism with a witness! Here is idolatry even without a mask: And he who can calmly hear, and digest such doctrine, hath forfeited his claim to rationality—an apostate from the order of manhood; and ought to be considered—as one, who hath not only given up the proper dignity of man, but sunk himself beneath the rank of animals, and contemptibly crawls through the world like a worm.

However, it matters very little now, what the king of England either says or does; he hath wickedly broken through every moral and human obligation, trampled nature and conscience beneath his feet; and by a steady and constitutional spirit of insolence and cruelty, procured for himself an universal hatred. It is *now* the interest of America to provide for herself. She hath already a large and young family, whom it is more her duty to take care of, than to be granting away her property, to support a power who is become a reproach to the names of men and Christians—*ye*, whose office it is to watch over the morals of a nation, of whatsoever sect or denomination ye are of, as well as ye, who are more immediately the guardians of the public liberty, if ye wish to preserve your native country uncontaminated by European corruption, ye must in secret wish a separation—But leaving the moral part to private reflection, I shall chiefly confine my farther remarks to the following heads.

First. That it is the interest of America to be separated from Britain.

Secondly. Which is the easiest and most practicable plan, *reconciliation or independance?* with some occasional remarks.

In support of the first, I could, if I judged it proper, produce the opinion of some of the ablest and most experienced men on this continent; and whose sentiments, on that head, are not yet publicly known. It is in reality a self-evident position: For no nation in a state of foreign dependance, limited in its commerce, and cramped and fettered in its legislative powers, can ever arrive at any material eminence. America doth not yet know what opulence is; and although the progress which she hath made stands unparalleled in the history of other nations, it is but childhood, compared with what she would be capable of arriving at, had she, as she ought to have, the legislative powers in her own hands. England is, at this time, proudly coveting what would do her no good, were she to accomplish it; and the Continent hesitating on a matter, which will be her final ruin if neglected. It is the commerce and not the conquest of America, by which England is to be benefited, and that would in a great measure continue, were the countries as independant of each other as France and Spain; because in many articles, neither can go to a better market. But it is the independance of this country of Britain or any other, which is now the main and only object worthy of contention, and which, like all other truths discovered by necessity, will appear clearer and stronger everyday.

First. Because it will come to that one time or other.

Secondly. Because, the longer it is delayed the harder it will be to accomplish.

I have frequently amused myself both in public and private companies, with silently remarking, the specious errors of those who speak without reflecting. And among the many which I have heard, the following seems the most general, viz. that had this rupture happened forty or fifty years hence, instead of *now*, the Continent would have been more able to have shaken off the dependance. To which I reply, that our military ability, *at this time*, arises from the experience gained in the last war, and which in forty or fifty years time, would have been totally extinct. The Continent, would not, by that time, have had a General, or even a military officer left; and we, or those who may succeed us, would have been as ignorant of martial matters as the ancient Indians: And this single position, closely attended to, will unanswerably prove, that the present time is preferable to all others. The argument turns thus—at the conclusion of the last war, we had experience, but wanted numbers; and forty or fifty years hence, we should have numbers, without experience; wherefore, the proper point of time, must be some particular point between the two extremes, in which a sufficiency of the former remains, and a proper increase of the latter is obtained: And that point of time is the present time.

The reader will pardon this digression, as it does not properly come under the head I first set out with, and to which I again return by the following position, viz.

Should affairs be patched up with Britain, and she to remain the governing and sovereign power of America, (which, as matters are now circumstanced, is giving up the point intirely) we shall deprive ourselves of the very means of sinking the debt we have, or may contract. The value of the back lands which some of the provinces are clandestinely deprived of, by the unjust extention of the limits of Canada, valued only at five pounds sterling per hundred acres, amount to upwards of twenty-five millions, Pennsylvania currency; and the quit-rents at one penny sterling per acre, to two millions yearly.

It is by the sale of those lands that the debt may be sunk, without burthen to any, and the quit-rent reserved thereon, will always lessen, and in time, will wholly support the yearly expence of government. It matters not how long the debt is in paying, so that the lands when sold be applied to the discharge of it, and for the execution of which, the Congress for the time being, will be the continental trustees.

I proceed now to the second head, viz. Which is the easiest and most practicable plan, *reconciliation* or *independance*; with some occasional remarks.

He who takes nature for his guide is not easily beaten out of his argument, and on that ground, I answer *generally—That independance being a single simple line, contained within ourselves; and reconciliation, a matter exceedingly perplexed and complicated, and in which, a treacherous capricious court is to interfere, gives the answer without a doubt.*

The present state of America is truly alarming to every man who is capable of reflexion. Without law, without government, without any other mode of power than what is founded on, and granted by courtesy. Held together by an unexampled concurrence of sentiment, which, is nevertheless subject to change, and which every secret enemy is endeavouring to dissolve. Our present condition, is, Legislation without law; wisdom without a plan; constitution without a name; and, what is strangely astonishing, perfect Independance contending for dependance. The instance is without a precedent; the case never existed before; and who can tell what may be the event? The property of no man is secure in the present unbraced system of things. The mind of the multitude is left at random, and seeing no fixed object before them, they pursue such as fancy or opinion starts. Nothing is criminal; there is no such thing as treason; wherefore, everyone thinks himself at liberty to act as he pleases. The Tories dared not have assembled offensively, had they known that their lives, by that act, were forfeited to the laws of the state. A line of distinction should be drawn, between, English soldiers taken in battle, and inhabitants of America taken in arms. The first are prisoners, but the latter traitors. The one forfeits his liberty, the other his head.

Notwithstanding our wisdom, there is a visible feebleness in some of our proceedings which gives encouragement to dissensions. The Continental Belt is too loosely buckled. And if something is not done in time, it will be too late to do anything, and we shall fall into a state, in which, neither *Reconciliation* nor *Independance* will be practicable. The king and his worthless adherents are got at their old game of dividing the Continent, and there are not wanting among us, Printers, who will be busy in spreading specious falsehoods. The artful and hypocritical letter which appeared a few months ago in two of the New-York papers, and likewise in two others, is an evidence that there are men who want either judgment or honesty.

It is easy getting into holes and corners and talking of reconciliation: But do such men seriously consider, how difficult the task is, and how dangerous it may prove, should the Continent divide thereon. Do they take within their view, all the various orders of men whose situation and circumstances, as well as their own, are to be considered therein. Do they put themselves in the place of the sufferer whose *all* is *already* gone, and of the soldier, who hath quitted *all* for the defence of his country. If their ill judged moderation be suited to their own private situations *only*, regardless of others, the event will convince them, that "they are reckoning without their Host."

Put us, say some, on the footing we were on in sixty-three: To which I answer, the request is not *now* in the power of Britain to comply with, neither will she propose it; but if it were, and even should be granted, I ask, as a reasonable question, By what means is such a corrupt and faithless court to be kept to its engagements? Another parliament, nay, even the present, may hereafter repeal the obligation, on the pretence, of its being violently obtained, or unwisely granted; and in that case, Where is our redress?—No going to law with nations; cannon are the barristers of Crowns; and the sword, not of justice, but of war, decides the suit. To be on the footing of sixty-three, it is not sufficient, that the laws only be put on the same state, but, that our circumstances, likewise, be put on the same state; Our burnt and destroyed towns repaired or built up, our private losses made good, our public debts (contracted for defence) discharged; otherwise, we shall be millions worse than we were at that enviable period. Such a request, had it been complied with a year ago, would have won the heart and soul of the Continent—but now it is too late, "The Rubicon is passed."

Besides, the taking up arms, merely to enforce the repeal of a pecuniary law, seems as unwarrantable by the divine law, and as repugnant to human feelings, as the taking up arms to enforce obedience thereto. The object, on either side, doth not justify the means; for the lives of men are too valuable to be cast away on such trifles. It is the violence which is done and threatened to our persons; the destruction of our property by an armed force; the invasion of our country by fire and sword, which conscientiously qualifies the use of arms: And the instant, in which such a mode of defence became necessary, all subjection to Britain ought to have ceased; and the independancy of America, should have been considered, as dating its æra from, and published by, *the first musket that was fired against her*. This line is a line of consistency; neither drawn by caprice, nor extended by ambition; but produced by a chain of events, of which the colonies were not the authors.

I shall conclude these remarks, with the following timely and well intended hints. We ought to reflect, that there are three different ways, by which an independancy may hereafter be effected; and that *one* of those *three*, will one day or other, be the fate of America, viz. By the legal voice of the people in Congress; by a military power; or by a mob: It may not always happen that our soldiers are citizens, and the multitude a body of reasonable men; virtue, as I have already remarked, is not hereditary, neither is it perpetual. Should an independancy be brought about by the first of those means, we have every opportunity and every encouragement before us, to form the noblest purest constitution on the face of the earth. We have it in our power to begin the world over again. A situation, similar to the present, hath not happened since the days of Noah until now. The birthday of a new world is at hand, and a race of men, perhaps as numerous as all Europe contains, are to receive their portion of freedom from the event of a few months. The Reflexion is awful—and in this point of view, How trifling, how ridiculous, do the little, paltry cavellings, of a few weak or interested men appear, when weighed against the business of a world.

Should we neglect the present favorable and inviting period, and an Independence be hereafter effected by any other means, we must charge the consequence to ourselves, or to those rather, whose narrow and prejudiced souls, are habitually opposing the measure, without either inquiring or reflecting. There are reasons to be given in support of Independance, which men should rather privately think of, than be publicly told of. We ought not now to be debating whether we shall be independant or not, but, anxious to accomplish it on a firm, secure, and honorable basis, and uneasy rather that it is not yet began upon. Everyday convinces us of its necessity. Even the Tories (if such beings yet remain among us) should, of all men, be the most solicitous to promote it; for, as the appointment of committees at first, protected them from popular rage, so, a wise and well established form of government, will be the only certain means of continuing it securely to them. *Wherefore*, if they have not virtue enough to be WHIGS, they ought to have prudence enough to wish for Independence.

In short, Independance is the only BOND that can tye and keep us together. We shall then see our object, and our ears will be legally shut against the schemes of an intriguing, as well, as a cruel enemy. We shall then too, be on a proper footing, to treat with Britain; for there is reason to conclude, that the pride of that court, will be less hurt by treating with the American states for terms of peace, than with those, whom she denominates, "rebellious subjects," for terms of accommodation. It is our delaying it that encourages her to hope for conquest, and our backwardness tends only to prolong the war. As we have, without any good effect therefrom, withheld our trade to obtain a redress of our grievances, let us *now* try the alternative, by *independantly* redressing them ourselves, and then offering to open the trade. The mercantile and reasonable part in England, will be still with us; because, peace *with* trade, is preferable to war *without* it. And if this offer be not accepted, other courts may be applied to.

On these grounds I rest the matter. And as no offer hath yet been made to refute the doctrine contained in the former editions of this pamphlet, it is a negative proof, that either the doctrine cannot be refuted, or, that the party in favour of it are too numerous to be opposed. WHEREFORE, instead of gazing at each other with suspicious or doubtful curiosity; let each of us, hold out to his neighbour the hearty hand of friendship, and unite in drawing a line, which, like an act of oblivion shall bury in forgetfulness every former dissension. Let the names of Whig and Tory be extinct; and let none other be heard among us, than those of *a good citizen, an open and resolute friend, and a virtuous supporter of the* RIGHTS *of* MANKIND *and of the* FREE AND INDEPENDANT STATES OF AMERICA.

To the Representatives of the Religious Society of the People called Quakers, or to so many of them as were concerned in publishing the late piece, entitled "*The Ancient Testimony and Principles* of the People called *Quakers* renewed, with Respect to the *King and Government*, and touching the *Commotions* now prevailing in these and other parts of *America* addressed to the *People in General*."

The Writer of this, is one of those few, who never dishonours religion either by ridiculing, or cavilling at any denomination whatsoever. To God, and not to man, are all men accountable on the score of religion. Wherefore, this epistle is not so properly addressed to you as a religious, but as a political body, dabbling in matters, which the professed Quietude of your Principles instruct you not to meddle with.

As you have, without a proper authority for so doing, put yourselves in the place of the whole body of the Quakers, so, the writer of this, in order to be on an equal rank with yourselves, is under the necessity, of putting himself in the place of all those, who, approve the very writings and principles, against which your testimony is directed: And he hath chosen this singular situation, in order, that you might discover in him that presumption of character which you cannot see in yourselves. For neither he nor you can have any claim or title to *Political Representation*.

When men have departed from the right way, it is no wonder that they stumble and fall. And it is evident from the manner in which ye have managed your testimony, that politics, (as a religious body of men) is not your proper Walk; for however well adapted it might appear to you, it is, nevertheless, a jumble of good and bad put unwisely together, and the conclusion drawn therefrom, both unnatural and unjust.

The two first pages, (and the whole doth not make four) we give you credit for, and expect the same civility from you, because the love and desire of peace is not confined to Quakerism, it is the natural, as well the religious wish of all denominations of men. And on this ground, as men labouring to establish an Independant Constitution of our own, do we exceed all others in our hope, end, and aim. *Our plan is peace forever.* We are tired of contention with Britain, and can see no real end to it but in a final separation. We act consistently, because for the sake of introducing an endless and uninterrupted peace, do we bear the evils and burthens of the present day. We are endeavoring, and will steadily continue to endeavour, to separate and dissolve a connexion which hath already filled our land with blood; and which, while the name of it remains, will be the fatal cause of future mischiefs to both countries.

We fight neither for revenge nor conquest; neither from pride nor passion; we are not insulting the world with our fleets and armies, nor ravaging the globe for plunder. Beneath the shade of our own vines are we attacked; in our own houses, and on our own lands, is the violence committed against us. We view our enemies in the character of Highwaymen and Housebreakers, and having no defence for ourselves in the civil law, are obliged to punish them by the military one, and apply the sword, in the very case, where you have before now, applied the halter—Perhaps we feel for the ruined and insulted sufferers in all and every part of the continent, with a degree of tenderness which hath not yet made its way into some of your bosoms. But be ye sure that ye mistake not the cause and ground of your Testimony. Call not coldness of soul, religion; nor put the *Bigot* in the place of the *Christian*.

O ye partial ministers of your own acknowledged principles. If the bearing arms be sinful, the first going to war must be more so, by all the difference between wilful attack and unavoidable defence. Wherefore, if ye really preach from conscience, and mean not to make a political hobby-horse of your religion, convince the world thereof, by proclaiming your doctrine to our enemies, *for they likewise bear* ARMS. Give us proof of your sincerity by publishing it at St. James's, to the commanders in chief at Boston, to the Admirals and Captains who are piratically ravaging our coasts, and to all the murdering miscreants who are acting in authority under HIM whom ye profess to serve. Had ye the honest soul of *Barclay* [3] ye would preach repentance to *your* king; Ye would tell the Royal Wretch his sins, and warn him of eternal ruin. Ye would not spend your partial invectives against the injured and the insulted only, but, like faithful ministers, would cry aloud and *spare none*. Say not that ye are persecuted, neither endeavour to make us the authors of that reproach, which, ye are bringing upon yourselves; for we testify unto all men, that we do not complain against you because ye are *Quakers*, but because ye pretend to *be* and are NOT Quakers.

Alas! it seems by the particular tendency of some part of your testimony, and other parts of your conduct, as if, all sin was reduced to, and comprehended in, *the act of bearing arms*, and that by the *people* only. Ye appear to us, to have mistaken party for conscience; because, the general tenor of your actions wants uniformity: And it is exceedingly difficult to us to give credit to many of your pretended scruples; because, we see them made by

---

3. "Thou hast tasted of prosperity and adversity; thou knowest what it is to be banished thy native country, to be over-ruled as well as to rule, and set upon the throne; and being *oppressed* thou hast reason to know how *hateful* the *oppressor* is both to God and man: If after all these warnings and advertisements, thou dost not turn unto the Lord with all thy heart, but forget him who remembered thee in thy distress, and give up thyself to follow lust and vanity, surely great will be thy condemnation.—Against which snare, as well as the temptation of those who may or do feed thee, and prompt thee to evil, the most excellent and prevalent remedy will be, to apply thyself to that light of Christ which shineth in thy conscience, and which neither can, nor will flatter thee, nor suffer thee to be at ease in thy sins."

—*Barclay's address to Charles II*

the same men, who, in the very instant that they are exclaiming against the mammon of this world, are nevertheless, hunting after it with a step as steady as Time, and an appetite as keen as Death.

The quotation which ye have made from Proverbs, in the third page of your testimony, that, "when a man's ways please the Lord, he maketh even his enemies to be at peace with him"; is very unwisely chosen on your part; because, it amounts to a proof, that the king's ways (whom ye are desirous of supporting) do *not* please the Lord, otherwise, his reign would be in peace.

I now proceed to the latter part of your testimony, and that, for which all the foregoing seems only an introduction, viz.

"It hath ever been our judgment and principle, since we were called to profess the light of Christ Jesus, manifested in our consciences unto this day, that the setting up and putting down kings and governments, is God's peculiar prerogative; for causes best known to himself: And that it is not our business to have any hand or contrivance therein; nor to be busy bodies above our station, much less to plot and contrive the ruin, or overturn of any of them, but to pray for the king, and safety of our nation, and good of all men: That we may live a peaceable and quiet life, in all godliness and honesty; *under the government which God is pleased to set over us.*"—If these are *really* your principles why do ye not abide by them? Why do ye not leave that, which ye call God's Work, to be managed by himself? These very principles instruct you to wait with patience and humility, for the event of all public measures, and to receive *that event* as the divine will towards you. *Wherefore*, what occasion is there for your *political testimony* if you fully believe what it contains: And the very publishing it proves, that either, ye do not believe what ye profess, or have not virtue enough to practise what ye believe.

The principles of Quakerism have a direct tendency to make a man the quiet and inoffensive subject of any, and every government *which is set over him*. And if the setting up and putting down of kings and governments is God's peculiar prerogative, he most certainly will not be robbed thereof by us; wherefore, the principle itself leads you to approve of everything, which ever happened, or may happen to kings as being his work. *Oliver Cromwell* thanks you. *Charles*, then, died not by the hands of man; and should the present Proud Imitator of him, come to the same untimely end, the writers and publishers of the Testimony, are bound, by the doctrine it contains, to applaud the fact. Kings are not taken away by miracles, neither are changes in governments brought about by any other means than such as are common and human; and such as we are now using. Even the dispersion of the Jews, though foretold by our Saviour, was effected by arms. Wherefore, as ye refuse to be the means on one side, ye ought not to be meddlers on the other; but to wait the issue in silence; and unless ye can produce divine authority, to prove, that the Almighty who hath created and placed this *new* world, at the greatest distance it could possibly stand, east and west, from every part of the old, doth, nevertheless, disapprove of its being independant of the corrupt and abandoned court of Britain, unless I say, ye can shew this, how can ye on the ground of your principles, justify the exciting and stirring up the people "firmly to unite in the *abhorrence* of all such *writings*, and *measures*, as evidence a desire and design to break off the *happy* connexion we have hitherto enjoyed, with the kingdom of Great-Britain, and our just and necessary subordination to the king, and those who are lawfully placed in authority under him." What a slap of the face is here! the men, who in the very paragraph before, have quietly and passively resigned up the ordering, altering, and disposal of kings and governments, into the hands of God, are now, recalling their principles, and putting in for a share of the business. Is it possible, that the conclusion, which is here justly quoted, can anyways follow from the doctrine laid down? The inconsistency is too glaring not to be seen; the absurdity too great not to be laughed at; and such as could only have been made by those, whose understandings were darkened by the narrow and crabby spirit of a despairing political party; for ye are not to be considered as the whole body of the Quakers but only as a factional and fractional part thereof.

Here ends the examination of your testimony; (which I call upon no man to abhor, as ye have done, but only to read and judge of fairly;) to which I subjoin the following remark; "That the setting up and putting down of kings," most certainly mean, the making him a king, who is yet not so, and the making him no king who is already one. And pray what hath this to do in the present case? We neither mean to *set up* nor to *put down*, neither to *make* nor to *unmake*, but to have nothing to *do* with them. Wherefore, your testimony in whatever light it is viewed serves only to dishonor your judgement, and for many other reasons had better have been let alone than published.

First, Because it tends to the decrease and reproach of all religion whatever, and is of the utmost danger to society, to make it a party in political disputes.

Secondly, Because it exhibits a body of men, numbers of whom disavow the publishing political testimonies, as being concerned therein and approvers thereof.

Thirdly, Because it hath a tendency to undo that continental harmony and friendship which yourselves by your late liberal and charitable donations hath lent a hand to establish; and the preservation of which, is of the utmost consequence to us all.

And here without anger or resentment I bid you farewell. Sincerely wishing, that as men and christians, ye may always fully and uninterruptedly enjoy every civil and religious right; and be, in your turn, the means of securing it to others; but that the example which ye have unwisely set, of mingling religion with politics, *may be disavowed and reprobated by every inhabitant of America.*

The Declaration of Independence

When in the Course of human events, it becomes necessary for one people to dissolve the political bands which have connected them with another, and to assume, among the Powers of the earth, the separate and equal station to which the Laws of Nature and of Nature's God entitle them, a decent respect to the opinions of mankind requires that they should declare the causes which impel them to the separation.

We hold these truths to be self-evident, that all men are created equal, that they are endowed by their Creator with certain unalienable Rights, that among these are Life, Liberty, and the pursuit of Happiness. That to secure these rights, Governments are instituted among Men, deriving their just powers from the consent of the governed, That whenever any Form of Government becomes destructive of these ends, it is the Right of the People to alter or to abolish it, and to institute new Government, laying its foundation on such principles and organizing its powers in such form, as to them shall seem most likely to effect their Safety and Happiness. Prudence, indeed, will dictate that Governments long established should not be changed for light and transient causes; and accordingly all experience hath shown, that mankind are more disposed to suffer, while evils are sufferable, than to right themselves by abolishing the forms to which they are accustomed. But when a long train of abuses and usurpations, pursuing invariably the same Object evinces a design to reduce them under absolute Despotism, it is their right, it is their duty, to throw off such Government, and to provide new Guards for their future security.—Such has been the patient sufferance of these Colonies; and such is now the necessity which constrains them to alter their former Systems of Government.

The history of the present King of Great Britain is a history of repeated injuries and usurpations, all having in direct object the establishment of an absolute Tyranny over these States. To prove this, let Facts be submitted to a candid world.

He has refused his Assent to Laws, the most wholesome and necessary for the public good.

He has forbidden his Governors to pass Laws of immediate and pressing importance, unless suspended in their operation till his Assent should be obtained; and when so suspended, he has utterly neglected to attend to them.

He has refused to pass other Laws for the accommodation of large districts of people, unless those people would relinquish the right of Representation in the Legislature, a right inestimable to them and formidable to tyrants only.

He has called together legislative bodies at places unusual, uncomfortable, and distant from the depository of their Public Records, for the sole purpose of fatiguing them into compliance with his measures.

He has dissolved Representative Houses repeatedly, for opposing with manly firmness his invasions on the rights of the people.

He has refused for a long time, after such dissolutions, to cause others to be elected; whereby the Legislative Powers, incapable of Annihilation, have returned to the People at large for their exercise; the State remaining in the mean time exposed to all the dangers of invasion from without, and convulsions within.

He has endeavoured to prevent the population of these States; for that purpose obstructing the Laws of Naturalization of Foreigners; refusing to pass others to encourage their migration hither, and raising the conditions of new Appropriations of Lands.

He has obstructed the Administration of Justice, by refusing his Assent to Laws for establishing Judiciary Powers.

He has made judges dependent on his Will alone, for the tenure of their offices, and the amount and payment of their salaries.

He has erected a multitude of New Offices, and sent hither swarms of Officers to harass our People, and eat out their substance.

He has kept among us, in times of peace, Standing Armies without the Consent of our legislatures.

He has affected to render the Military independent of and superior to the Civil Power.

He has combined with others to subject us to a jurisdiction foreign to our constitution, and unacknowledged by our laws; giving his Assent to their Acts of pretended legislation:

For quartering large bodies of armed troops among us:

For protecting them, by a mock Trial, from Punishment for any Murders which they should commit on the Inhabitants of these States:

For cutting off our Trade with all parts of the world:

For imposing taxes on us without our Consent:

For depriving us, in many cases, of the benefits of Trial by Jury:

For transporting us beyond Seas to be tried for pretended offences:

For abolishing the free System of English Laws in a neighbouring Province, establishing therein an Arbitrary government, and enlarging its Boundaries so as to render it at once an example and fit instrument for introducing the same absolute rule into these Colonies:

For taking away our Charters, abolishing our most valuable Laws, and altering fundamentally the Forms of our Governments:

For suspending our own Legislatures, and declaring themselves invested with Power to legislate for us in all cases whatsoever.

He has abdicated Government here, by declaring us out of his Protection and waging War against us.

He has plundered our seas, ravaged our Coasts, burnt our towns, and destroyed the lives of our people.

He is at this time transporting large armies of foreign mercenaries to complete the works of death, desolation and tyranny, already begun with circumstances of Cruelty & perfidy scarcely paralleled in the most barbarous ages, and totally unworthy of the Head of a civilized nation.

He has constrained our fellow Citizens taken Captive on the high Seas to bear Arms against their Country, to become the executioners of their friends and Brethren, or to fall themselves by their Hands.

He has excited domestic insurrections amongst us, and has endeavoured to bring on the inhabitants of our frontiers, the merciless Indian Savages, whose known rule of warfare, is an undistinguished destruction of all ages, sexes and conditions.

In every stage of these Oppressions We have Petitioned for Redress in the most humble terms: Our repeated Petitions have been answered only by repeated injury. A Prince, whose character is thus marked by every act which may define a Tyrant, is unfit to be the ruler of a free People.

Nor have We been wanting in attention to our British brethren. We have warned them from time to time of attempts by their legislature to extend an unwarrantable jurisdiction over us. We have reminded them of the circumstances of our emigration and settlement here. We have appealed to their native justice and magnanimity, and we have conjured them by the ties of our common kindred to disavow these usurpations, which would inevitably interrupt our connections and correspondence. They too have been deaf to the voice of justice and of consanguinity. We must, therefore, acquiesce in the necessity, which denounces our Separation, and hold them, as we hold the rest of mankind, Enemies in War, in Peace Friends.

We, therefore, the Representatives of the United States of America, in General Congress, Assembled, appealing to the Supreme Judge of the world for the rectitude of our intentions, do, in the Name, and by the Authority of the good People of these Colonies, solemnly publish and declare, That these United Colonies are, and of Right ought to be Free and Independent States; that they are Absolved from all Allegiance to the British Crown, and that all political connection between them and the State of Great Britain, is and ought to be totally dissolved; and that as Free and Independent States, they have full Power to levy War, conclude Peace, contract Alliances, establish Commerce, and to do all other Acts and Things which Independent States may of right do. And for the support of this Declaration, with a firm reliance on the Protection of Divine Providence, we mutually pledge to each other our Lives, our Fortunes and our sacred Honor.

The Articles of Confederation

To all to whom these Presents shall come, we, the undersigned Delegates of the States affixed to our Names send greeting. Whereas the Delegates of the United States of America in Congress assembled did on the fifteenth day of November in the year of our Lord One Thousand Seven Hundred and Seventy seven, and in the Second Year of the Independence of America agree to certain articles of Confederation and perpetual Union between the States of Newhampshire, Massachusetts-bay, Rhodeisland and Providence Plantations, Connecticut, New York, New Jersey, Pennsylvania, Delaware, Maryland, Virginia, North Carolina, South Carolina, and Georgia in the Words following, viz. "Articles of Confederation and perpetual Union between the States of Newhampshire, Massachusetts-bay, Rhodeisland and Providence Plantations, Connecticut, New York, New Jersey, Pennsylvania, Delaware, Maryland, Virginia, North Carolina, South Carolina, and Georgia.

Article I. The Stile of this confederacy shall be, "The United States of America."

Article II. Each state retains its sovereignty, freedom and independence, and every Power, Jurisdiction and right, which is not by this confederation expressly delegated to the United States, in Congress assembled.

Article III. The said states hereby severally enter into a firm league of friendship with each other, for their common defence, the security of their Liberties, and their mutual and general welfare, binding themselves to assist each other, against all force offered to, or attacks made upon them, or any of them, on account of religion, sovereignty, trade, or any other pretence whatever.

Article IV. The better to secure and perpetuate mutual friendship and intercourse among the people of the different states in this union, the free inhabitants of each of these states, paupers, vagabonds and fugitives from Justice excepted, shall be entitled to all privileges and immunities of free citizens in the several states; and the people of each state shall have free ingress and regress to and from any other state, and shall enjoy therein all the privileges of trade and commerce, subject to the same duties, impositions and restrictions as the inhabitants thereof respectively, provided that such restrictions shall not extend so far as to prevent the removal of property imported into any state, to any other State of which the Owner is an inhabitant; provided also that no imposition, duties or restriction shall be laid by any state, on the property of the United States, or either of them.

If any Person guilty of, or charged with, treason, felony, or other high misdemeanor in any state, shall flee from Justice, and be found in any of the United States, he shall upon demand of the Governor or executive power of the state from which he fled, be delivered up, and removed to the state having jurisdiction of his offence.

Full faith and credit shall be given in each of these states to the records, acts and judicial proceedings of the courts and magistrates of every other state.

Article V. For the more convenient management of the general interests of the United States, delegates shall be annually appointed in such manner as the legislature of each state shall direct, to meet in Congress on the first Monday in November, in every year, with a power reserved to each state to recall its delegates, or any of them, at anytime within the year, and to send others in their stead, for the remainder of the Year.

No State shall be represented in Congress by less than two, nor by more than seven Members; and no person shall be capable of being delegate for more than three years, in any term of six years; nor shall any person, being a delegate, be capable of holding any office under the United States, for which he, or another for his benefit receives any salary, fees or emolument of any kind.

Each State shall maintain its own delegates in a meeting of the states, and while they act as members of the committee of the states.

In determining questions in the United States, in Congress assembled, each state shall have one vote.

Freedom of speech and debate in Congress shall not be impeached or questioned in any Court, or place out of Congress, and the members of congress shall be protected in their persons from arrests and imprisonments, during the time of their going to and from, and attendance on congress, except for treason, felony, or breach of the peace.

Article VI. No State, without the Consent of the United States, in congress assembled, shall send any embassy to, or receive any embassy from, or enter into any conferrence, agreement, alliance, or treaty, with any King prince or state; nor shall any person holding any office of profit or trust under the United States, or any of them, accept of any present, emolument, office, or title of any kind whatever, from any king, prince, or foreign state; nor shall the United States, in congress assembled, or any of them, grant any title of nobility.

No two or more states shall enter into any treaty, confederation, or alliance whatever between them, without the consent of the United States, in congress assembled, specifying accurately the purposes for which the same is to be entered into, and how long it shall continue.

No State shall lay any imposts or duties, which may interfere with any stipulations in treaties, entered into by the United States in congress assembled, with any king, prince, or State, in pursuance of any treaties already proposed by congress, to the courts of France and Spain.

No vessels of war shall be kept up in time of peace, by any state, except such number only, as shall be deemed necessary by the United States, in congress assembled, for the defence of such state, or its trade; nor shall anybody of forces be kept up, by any state, in time of peace, except such number only as, in the judgment of the United States, in congress assembled, shall be deemed requisite to garrison the forts necessary for the defence of such state; but every state shall always keep up a well regulated and disciplined militia, sufficiently armed and accoutred, and shall provide and constantly have ready for use, in public stores, a due number of field pieces and tents, and a proper quantity of arms, ammunition, and camp equipage.

No State shall engage in any war without the consent of the United States in congress assembled, unless such State be actually invaded by enemies, or shall have received certain advice of a resolution being formed by some nation of Indians to invade such State, and the danger is so imminent as not to admit of a delay till the United States in congress assembled, can be consulted: nor shall any state grant commissions to any ships or vessels of war, nor letters of marque or reprisal, except it be after a declaration of war by the United States in congress assembled, and then only against the kingdom or State, and the subjects thereof, against which war has been so declared, and under such regulations as shall be established by the United States in congress assembled, unless such state be infested by pirates, in which case vessels of war may be fitted out for that occasion, and kept so long as the danger shall continue, or until the United States in congress assembled shall determine otherwise.

Article VII. When land forces are raised by any state, for the common defence, all officers of or under the rank of colonel, shall be appointed by the legislature of each state respectively by whom such forces shall be raised, or in such manner as such state shall direct, and all vacancies shall be filled up by the state which first made appointment.

Article VIII. All charges of war, and all other expenses that shall be incurred for the common defence or general welfare, and allowed by the United States in congress assembled, shall be defrayed out of a common treasury, which shall be supplied by the several states, in proportion to the value of all land within each state, granted to or surveyed for any Person, as such land and the buildings and improvements thereon shall be estimated, according to such mode as the United States, in congress assembled, shall, from time to time, direct and appoint. The taxes for paying that proportion shall be laid and levied by the authority and direction of the legislatures of the several states within the time agreed upon by the United States in congress assembled.

Article IX. The United States, in congress assembled, shall have the sole and exclusive right and power of determining on peace and war, except in the cases mentioned in the sixth article of sending and receiving ambassadors entering into treaties and alliances, provided that no treaty of commerce shall be made, whereby the legislative power of the respective states shall be restrained from imposing such imposts and duties on foreigners, as their own people are subjected to, or from prohibiting the exportation or importation of any species of goods or commodities whatsoever of establishing rules for deciding, in all cases, what captures on land or water shall be legal, and in what manner prizes taken by land or naval forces in the service of the United States, shall be divided or appropriated of granting letters of marque and reprisal in times of peace appointing courts for the trial of piracies and felonies committed on the high seas; and establishing courts; for receiving and determining finally appeals in all cases of captures; provided that no member of congress shall be appointed a judge of any of the said courts.

The United States, in congress assembled, shall also be the last resort on appeal, in all disputes and differences now subsisting, or that hereafter may arise between two or more states concerning boundary, jurisdiction, or any other cause whatever; which authority shall always be exercised in the manner following. Whenever the legislative or executive authority, or lawful agent of any state in controversy with another, shall present a petition to congress, stating the matter in question, and praying for a hearing, notice thereof shall be given, by order of congress, to the legislative or executive authority of the other state in controversy, and a day assigned for the appearance of the parties by their lawful agents, who shall then be directed to appoint, by joint consent, commissioners or judges to constitute a court for hearing and determining the matter in question: but if they cannot agree, congress shall name three persons out of each of the United States, and from the list of such persons each party shall alternately strike out one, the petitioners beginning, until the number shall be reduced to thirteen; and from that number not less than seven, nor more than nine names, as congress shall direct, shall, in the presence of congress, be drawn out by lot, and the persons whose names shall be so drawn, or any five of them, shall be commissioners or judges, to hear and finally determine the controversy, so always as a major part of the judges, who shall hear the cause, shall agree in the determination: and if either party shall neglect to attend at the day appointed, without showing reasons which congress shall judge sufficient, or being present, shall refuse to strike, the congress shall proceed to nominate three persons out of each State, and the secretary of congress shall strike in behalf of such party absent or refusing; and the judgment and sentence of the court, to be appointed in the manner before prescribed, shall be final and conclusive; and if any of the parties shall refuse to submit to the authority of such court, or to appear or defend their claim or cause, the court shall nevertheless proceed to pronounce sentence, or judgment, which shall in like manner be final and decisive; the judgment or sentence and other proceedings being in either case transmitted to congress, and lodged among the acts of congress, for the security of the parties concerned: provided that every commissioner, before he sits in judgment, shall take an oath to be administered by one of the judges of the supreme or superior court of the State where the cause shall be tried, "well and truly to hear and determine the matter in question, according to the best of his judgment, without favour, affection, or hope of reward: "provided, also, that no State shall be deprived of territory for the benefit of the United States.

All controversies concerning the private right of soil claimed under different grants of two or more states, whose jurisdictions as they may respect such lands, and the states which passed such grants are adjusted, the said grants or either of them being at the same time claimed to have originated antecedent to such settlement of jurisdiction, shall, on the petition of either party to the congress of the United States, be finally determined, as near as may be, in the same manner as is before prescribed for deciding disputes respecting territorial jurisdiction between different states.

The United States, in congress assembled, shall also have the sole and exclusive right and power of regulating the alloy and value of coin struck by their own authority, or by that of the respective states fixing the standard of weights and measures throughout the United States regulating the trade and managing all affairs with the Indians, not members of any of the states; provided that the legislative right of any state, within its own limits, be not infringed or violated establishing and regulating post-offices from one state to another, throughout all the United States, and exacting such postage on the papers passing through the same, as may be requisite to defray the expenses of the said office appointing all officers of the land forces in the service of the United States, excepting regimental officers appointing all the officers of the naval forces, and commissioning all officers whatever in the service of the United States; making rules for the government and regulation of the said land and naval forces, and directing their operations.

The United States, in congress assembled, shall have authority to appoint a committee, to sit in the recess of congress, to be denominated, "A Committee of the States," and to consist of one delegate from each State; and to appoint such other committees and civil officers as may be necessary for managing the general affairs of the United States under their direction to appoint one of their number to preside; provided that no person be allowed to serve in the office of president more than one year in any term of three years; to ascertain the necessary sums of money to be raised for the service of the United States, and to appropriate and apply the same for defraying the public expenses; to borrow money or emit bills on the credit of the United States, transmitting every half year to the respective states an account of the sums of money so borrowed or emitted, to build and equip a navy to agree upon the number of land forces, and to make requisitions from each state for its quota, in proportion to the number of white inhabitants in such state, which requisition shall be binding; and thereupon the legislature of each state shall appoint the regimental officers, raise the men, and clothe, arm, and equip them, in a soldier-like manner, at the expense of the United States; and the officers and men so clothed, armed, and equipped, shall march to the place appointed, and within the time agreed on by the United States, in congress assembled; but if the United States, in congress assembled, shall, on consideration of circumstances, judge proper that any state should not raise men, or should raise a smaller number than its quota, and that any other state should raise a greater number of men than the quota thereof, such extra number shall be raised, officered, clothed, armed, and equipped in the same manner as the quota of such state, unless the legislature of such state shall judge that such extra number cannot be safely spared out of the same, in which case they shall raise, officer, clothe, arm, and equip, as many of such extra number as they judge can be safely spared. And the officers and men so clothed, armed, and equipped, shall march to the place appointed, and within the time agreed on by the United States in congress assembled.

The United States, in congress assembled, shall never engage in a war, nor grant letters of marque and reprisal in time of peace, nor enter into any treaties or alliances, nor coin money, nor regulate the value thereof nor ascertain the sums and expenses necessary for the defence and welfare of the United States, or any of them, nor emit bills, nor borrow money on the credit of the United States, nor appropriate money, nor agree upon the number of vessels of war to be built or purchased, or the number of land or sea forces to be raised, nor appoint a commander in chief of the army or navy, unless nine states assent to the same, nor shall a question on any other point, except for adjourning from day today, be determined, unless by the votes of a majority of the United States in congress assembled.

The congress of the United States shall have power to adjourn to anytime within the year, and to any place within the United States, so that no period of adjournment be for a longer duration than the space of six Months, and shall publish the Journal of their proceedings monthly, except such parts thereof relating to treaties, alliances, or military operations, as in their judgment require secrecy; and the yeas and nays of the delegates of each State, on any question, shall be entered on the Journal, when it is desired by any delegate; and the delegates of a State, or any of them, at his or their request, shall be furnished with a transcript of the said Journal, except such parts as are above excepted, to lay before the legislatures of the several states.

Article X. The committee of the states, or any nine of them, shall be authorized to execute, in the recess of congress, such of the powers of congress as the United States, in congress assembled, by the consent of nine states, shall, from time to time, think expedient to vest them with; provided that no power be delegated to the said committee, for the exercise of which, by the articles of confederation, the voice of nine states, in the congress of the United States assembled, is requisite.

Article XI. Canada acceding to this confederation, and joining in the measures of the United States, shall be admitted into, and entitled to all the advantages of this union: but no other colony shall be admitted into the same, unless such admission be agreed to by nine states.

Article XII. All bills of credit emitted, monies borrowed, and debts contracted by or under the authority of congress, before the assembling of the United States, in pursuance of the present confederation, shall be deemed and considered as a charge against the United States, for payment and satisfaction whereof the said United States and the public faith are hereby solemnly pledged.

Article XIII. Every State shall abide by the determinations of the United States, in congress assembled, on all questions which by this confederation are submitted to them. And the Articles of this confederation shall be inviolably observed by every state, and the union shall be perpetual; nor shall any alteration at anytime hereafter be made in any of them, unless such alteration be agreed to in a congress of the United States, and be afterwards confirmed by the legislatures of every state.

And Whereas it hath pleased the Great Governor of the World to incline the hearts of the legislatures we respectively represent in congress, to approve of, and to authorize us to ratify the said articles of confederation and perpetual union, Know Ye, that we, the undersigned delegates, by virtue of the power and authority to us given for that purpose, do, by these presents, in the name and in behalf of our respective constituents, fully and entirely ratify and confirm each and every of the said articles of confederation and perpetual union, and all and singular the matters and things therein contained. And we do further solemnly plight and engage the faith of our respective constituents, that they shall abide by the determinations of the United States in congress assembled, on all questions, which by the said confederation are submitted to them. And that the articles thereof shall be inviolably observed by the states we respectively represent, and that the union shall be perpetual. In Witness whereof, we have hereunto set our hands, in Congress. Done at Philadelphia, in the State of Pennsylvania, the ninth Day of July, in the Year of our Lord one Thousand seven Hundred and Seventy eight, and in the third year of the Independence of America.

The United States' Constitution
by Founding Fathers

We the people of the United States, in Order to form a more perfect Union, establish Justice, insure domestic Tranquility, provide for the common defence, promote the general Welfare, and secure the Blessings of Liberty to ourselves and our Posterity, do ordain and establish this Constitution for the United States of America.

Article 1

SECTION 1. ALL LEGISLATIVE POWERS HEREIN granted shall be vested in a Congress of the United States, which shall consist of a Senate and House of Representatives.

Section 2. The House of Representatives shall be composed of Members chosen every second Year by the People of the several States, and the electors in each State shall have the qualifications requisite for electors of the most numerous branch of the State legislature.

No Person shall be a Representative who shall not have attained to the Age of twenty five Years, and been seven Years a citizen of the United States, and who shall not, when elected, be an Inhabitant of that State in which he shall be chosen.

Representatives and direct Taxes shall be apportioned among the several States which may be included within this Union, according to their respective Numbers, which shall be determined by adding to the whole number of free Persons, including those bound to Service for a Term of Years, and excluding Indians not taxed, three fifths of all other Persons. The actual Enumeration shall be made within three Years after the first Meeting of the Congress of the United States, and within every subsequent Term of ten Years, in such Manner as they shall by law Direct. The number of Representatives shall not exceed one for every thirty Thousand, but each State shall have at least one Representative; and until such enumeration shall be made, the State of New Hampshire shall be entitled to chuse three, Massachusetts eight, Rhode Island and Providence Plantations one, Connecticut five, New York six, New Jersey four, Pennsylvania eight, Delaware one, Maryland six, Virginia ten, North Carolina five, South Carolina five, and Georgia three.

When vacancies happen in the Representation from any State, the Executive Authority thereof shall issue Writs of Election to fill such Vacancies.

The House of Representatives shall chuse their Speaker and other Officers; and shall have the sole Power of Impeachment.

Section 3. The Senate of the United States shall be composed of two Senators from each State, chosen by the legislature thereof, for six Years; and each Senator shall have one Vote.

Immediately after they shall be assembled in Consequence of the first Election, they shall be divided as equally as may be into three Classes. The Seats of the Senators of the first Class shall be vacated at the expiration of the second Year, of the second Class at the expiration of the fourth Year, and of the third Class at the expiration of the sixth Year, so that one third may be chosen every second Year; and if vacancies happen by Resignation, or otherwise, during the recess of the Legislature of any State, the Executive thereof may make temporary Appointments until the next meeting of the Legislature, which shall then fill such Vacancies.

No person shall be a Senator who shall not have attained to the Age of thirty Years, and been nine Years a Citizen of the United States, and who shall not, when elected, be an Inhabitant of that State for which he shall be chosen.

The Vice-President of the United States shall be President of the Senate, but shall have no Vote, unless they be equally divided.

The Senate shall choose their other Officers, and also a President pro tempore, in the Absence of the Vice-President, or when he shall exercise the Office of President of the United States.

The Senate shall have the sole Power to try all Impeachments. When sitting for that Purpose, they shall be on Oath or Affirmation. When the President of the United States is tried, the Chief Justice shall preside: And no Person shall be convicted without the Concurrence of two thirds of the Members present.

Judgment in cases of Impeachment shall not extend further than to removal from Office, and disqualification to hold and enjoy any Office of honor, Trust or Profit under the United States: but the Party convicted shall nevertheless be liable and subject to Indictment, Trial, Judgment and Punishment, according to Law.

Section 4. The Times, Places and Manner of holding Elections for Senators and Representatives, shall be prescribed in each State by the Legislature thereof; but the Congress may at any time by Law make or alter such Regulations, except as to the Places of chusing Senators.

The Congress shall assemble at least once in every Year, and such Meeting shall be on the first Monday in December, unless they shall by law appoint a different Day.

Section 5. Each House shall be the Judge of the Elections, Returns and Qualifications of its own Members, and a Majority of each shall constitute a Quorum to do Business; but a smaller Number may adjourn from day today, and may be authorized to compel the Attendance of absent Members, in such Manner, and under such Penalties as each House may provide.

Each house may determine the Rules of its Proceedings, punish its Members for disorderly Behavior, and, with the Concurrence of two-thirds, expel a Member.

Each house shall keep a Journal of its Proceedings, and from time to time publish the same, excepting such Parts as may in their Judgment require Secrecy; and the Yeas and Nays of the Members of either House on any question shall, at the Desire of one fifth of those Present, be entered on the Journal.

Neither House, during the Session of Congress, shall, without the Consent of the other, adjourn for more than three days, nor to any other Place than that in which the two Houses shall be sitting.

Section 6. The Senators and Representatives shall receive a Compensation for their Services, to be ascertained by Law, and paid out of the Treasury of the United States. They shall in all Cases, except Treason, Felony and Breach of the Peace, be privileged from Arrest during their Attendance at the Session of their respective Houses, and in going to and returning from the same; and for any Speech or Debate in either House, they shall not be questioned in any other Place.

No Senator or Representative shall, during the Time for which he was elected, be appointed to any civil Office under the authority of the United States, which shall have been created, or the Emoluments whereof shall have been increased during such time; and no Person holding any Office under the United States, shall be a Member of either House during his Continuance in Office.

Section 7. All Bills for raising Revenue shall originate in the House of Representatives; but the Senate may propose or concur with Amendments as on other Bills.

Every Bill which shall have passed the House of Representatives and the Senate, shall, before it become a Law, be presented to the President of the United States; If he approve he shall sign it, but if not he shall return it, with his Objections to that House in which it shall have originated, who shall enter the Objections at large on their Journal, and proceed to reconsider it. If after such Reconsideration two thirds of that house shall agree to pass the

Bill, it shall be sent, together with the Objections, to the other House, by which it shall likewise be reconsidered, and if approved by two thirds of that House, it shall become a law. But in all such Cases the Votes of both Houses shall be determined by Yeas and Nays, and the Names of the Persons voting for and against the Bill shall be entered on the Journal of each House respectively. If any Bill shall not be returned by the President within ten Days (Sundays excepted) after it shall have been presented to him, the Same shall be a Law, in like Manner as if he had signed it, unless the Congress by their Adjournment prevent its Return, in which case it shall not be a Law.

Every Order, Resolution, or Vote to which the Concurrence of the Senate and House of Representatives may be necessary (except on a question of Adjournment) shall be presented to the President of the United States; and before the Same shall take Effect, shall be approved by him, or being disapproved by him, shall be repassed by two thirds of the Senate and House of Representatives, according to the Rules and Limitations prescribed in the Case of a Bill.

Section 8. The Congress shall have Power to lay and collect Taxes, Duties, Imposts and Excises, to pay the Debts and provide for the common Defence and general Welfare of the United States; but all Duties, Imposts and Excises shall be uniform throughout the United States;

To borrow Money on the credit of the United States;

To regulate Commerce with foreign Nations, and among the several States, and with the Indian Tribes;

To establish an uniform Rule of Naturalization, and uniform Laws on the subject of Bankruptcies throughout the United States;

To coin Money, regulate the Value thereof, and of foreign Coin, and fix the Standard of Weights and Measures;

To provide for the Punishment of counterfeiting the Securities and current Coin of the United States;

To establish Post Offices and Post Roads;

To promote the Progress of Science and useful Arts, by securing for limited Times to Authors and Inventors the exclusive Right to their respective Writings and Discoveries;

To constitute Tribunals inferior to the supreme Court;

To define and punish Piracies and Felonies committed on the high Seas, and Offenses against the Law of Nations;

To declare War, grant Letters of Marque and Reprisal, and make Rules concerning Captures on Land and Water;

To raise and support Armies, but no Appropriation of Money to that Use shall be for a longer term than two Years;

To provide and maintain a Navy;

To make Rules for the Government and Regulation of the land and naval Forces;

To provide for calling forth the Militia to execute the Laws of the Union, suppress Insurrections and repel Invasions;

To provide for organizing, arming, and disciplining, the Militia, and for governing such Part of them as may be employed in the Service of the United States, reserving to the States respectively, the Appointment of the Officers, and the Authority of training the militia according to the discipline prescribed by Congress;

To exercise exclusive Legislation in all Cases whatsoever, over such District (not exceeding ten Miles square) as may, by Cession of particular States, and the Acceptance of Congress, become the Seat of the Government of the United States, and to exercise like Authority over all Places purchased by the Consent of the Legislature of the State in which the Same shall be, for the Erection of Forts, Magazines, Arsenals, Dockyards, and other needful Buildings;—And

To make all Laws which shall be necessary and proper for carrying into Execution the foregoing Powers, and all other Powers vested by this Constitution in the Government of the United States, or in any Department or Officer thereof.

Section 9. The Migration or Importation of such Persons as any of the States now existing shall think proper to admit, shall not be prohibited by the Congress prior to the Year one thousand eight hundred and eight, but a Tax or Duty may be imposed on such Importation, not exceeding ten dollars for each Person.

The Privilege of the Writ of Habeas Corpus shall not be suspended, unless when in Cases of Rebellion or Invasion the public Safety may require it.

No Bill of Attainder or ex post facto Law shall be passed.

No Capitation, or other direct, Tax shall be laid, unless in Proportion to the Census or Enumeration herein before directed to be taken.

No Tax or Duty shall be laid on Articles exported from any State.

No Preference shall be given by any Regulation of Commerce or Revenue to the Ports of one State over those of another: nor shall Vessels bound to, or from, one State, be obliged to enter, clear, or pay Duties in another.

No Money shall be drawn from the Treasury, but in Consequence of Appropriations made by Law; and a regular Statement and Account of the Receipts and Expenditures of all public Money shall be published from time to time.

No Title of Nobility shall be granted by the United States; and no Person holding any Office of Profit or Trust under them, shall, without the Consent of the Congress, accept of any present, Emolument, Office, or Title, of any kind whatever, from any King, Prince, or foreign State.

Section 10. No State shall enter into any Treaty, Alliance, or Confederation; grant Letters of Marque and Reprisal; coin Money; emit Bills of Credit; make any Thing but gold and silver Coin a Tender in Payment of Debts; pass any Bill of Attainder, ex post facto Law, or Law impairing the Obligation of Contracts, or grant any Title of Nobility.

No State shall, without the Consent of the Congress, lay any Imposts or Duties on Imports or Exports, except what may be absolutely necessary for executing it's inspection Laws: and the net Produce of all Duties and Imposts, laid by any State on Imports or Exports, shall be for the Use of the Treasury of the United States; and all such Laws shall be subject to the Revision and Controul of the Congress.

No State shall, without the Consent of Congress, lay any Duty of Tonnage, keep Troops, or Ships of War in time of Peace, enter into any Agreement or Compact with another State, or with a foreign Power, or engage in War, unless actually invaded, or in such imminent Danger as will not admit of delay.

Article 2

SECTION 1. THE EXECUTIVE POWER SHALL be vested in a President of the United States of America. He shall hold his Office during the Term of four Years, and, together with the Vice President chosen for the same Term, be elected, as follows:

Each State shall appoint, in such Manner as the Legislature thereof may direct, a Number of Electors, equal to the whole Number of Senators and Representatives to which the State may be entitled in the Congress: but no Senator or Representative, or Person holding an Office of Trust or Profit under the United States, shall be appointed an Elector.

The Electors shall meet in their respective States, and vote by Ballot for two Persons, of whom one at least shall not be an Inhabitant of the same State with themselves. And they shall make a List of all the Persons voted for, and of the Number of Votes for each; which List they shall sign and certify, and transmit sealed to the Seat of the Government of the United States, directed to the President of the Senate. The President of the Senate shall, in the Presence of the Senate and House of Representatives, open all the Certificates, and the Votes shall then be counted. The Person having the greatest Number of Votes shall be the President, if such Number be a Majority of the whole Number of Electors appointed; and if there be more than one who have such Majority, and have an equal Number of votes, then the House of Representatives shall immediately chuse by Ballot one of them for President; and if no Person have a Majority, then from the five highest on the List the said House shall in like Manner chuse the President. But in chusing the President, the Votes shall be taken by States, the Representation from each State having one Vote; a Quorum for this Purpose shall consist of a Member or Members from two thirds of the States, and a Majority of all the States shall be necessary to a Choice. In every Case, after the Choice of the President, the Person having the greatest Number of Votes of the Electors shall be the Vice President. But if there should remain two or more who have equal Votes, the Senate shall chuse from them by Ballot the Vice President.

The Congress may determine the Time of chusing the Electors, and the Day on which they shall give their Votes; which Day shall be the same throughout the United States.

No Person except a natural born Citizen, or a Citizen of the United States, at the time of the Adoption of this Constitution, shall be eligible to the Office of President; neither shall any Person be eligible to that Office who shall not have attained to the Age of thirty five Years, and been fourteen Years a Resident within the United States.

In Case of the Removal of the President from Office, or of his Death, Resignation, or Inability to discharge the Powers and Duties of the said Office, the Same shall devolve on the Vice President, and the Congress may by Law provide for the Case of Removal, Death, Resignation or Inability, both of the President and Vice President, declaring what Officer shall then act as President, and such Officer shall act accordingly, until the Disability be removed, or a President shall be elected.

The President shall, at stated Times, receive for his Services, a Compensation, which shall neither be increased nor diminished during the Period for which he shall have been elected, and he shall not receive within that Period any other Emolument from the United States, or any of them.

Before he enter on the Execution of his Office, he shall take the following Oath or Affirmation:—"I do solemnly swear (or affirm) that I will faithfully execute the Office of President of the United States, and will to the best of my Ability, preserve, protect and defend the Constitution of the United States."

Section 2. The President shall be Commander in Chief of the Army and Navy of the United States, and of the Militia of the several States, when called into the actual Service of the United States; he may require the Opinion, in writing, of the principal Officer in each of the executive Departments, upon any Subject relating to the Duties of their respective Offices, and he shall have Power to grant Reprieves and Pardons for Offenses against the United States, except in Cases of impeachment.

He shall have Power, by and with the Advice and Consent of the Senate, to make Treaties, provided two thirds of the Senators present concur; and he shall nominate, and by and with the Advice and Consent of the Senate, shall appoint Ambassadors, other public Ministers and Consuls, Judges of the supreme Court, and all other Officers of the United States, whose Appointments are not herein otherwise provided for, and which shall be established by Law: but the Congress may by Law vest the Appointment of such inferior Officers, as they think proper, in the President alone, in the Courts of Law, or in the Heads of Departments.

The President shall have Power to fill up all Vacancies that may happen during the Recess of the Senate, by granting Commissions which shall expire at the End of their next session.

Section 3. He shall from time to time give to the Congress Information of the State of the Union, and recommend to their Consideration such Measures as he shall judge necessary and expedient; he may, on extraordinary Occasions, convene both Houses, or either of them, and in Case of Disagreement between them, with Respect to the Time of Adjournment, he may adjourn them to such Time as he shall think proper; he shall receive Ambassadors and other public Ministers; he shall take Care that the Laws be faithfully executed, and shall Commission all the Officers of the United States.

Section 4. The President, Vice President and all civil Officers of the United States, shall be removed from Office on Impeachment for, and Conviction of, Treason, Bribery, or other high Crimes and Misdemeanors.

Article Three

SECTION 1. THE JUDICIAL POWER OF the United States, shall be vested in one supreme Court, and in such inferior Courts as the Congress may from time to time ordain and establish. The Judges, both of the supreme and inferior Courts, shall hold their Offices during good behavior, and shall, at stated Times, receive for their

Services, a Compensation, which shall not be diminished during their Continuance in Office.

Section 2. The judicial Power shall extend to all Cases, in Law and Equity, arising under this Constitution, the Laws of the United States, and Treaties made, or which shall be made, under their Authority;—to all Cases affecting Ambassadors, other public Ministers and Consuls;—to all Cases of admiralty and maritime Jurisdiction;—to Controversies to which the United States shall be a Party;—to Controversies between two or more States;—between a State and Citizens of another State;—between Citizens of different States;—between Citizens of the same State claiming Lands under Grants of different States, and between a State, or the Citizens thereof, and foreign States, Citizens or Subjects.

In all cases affecting Ambassadors, other public Ministers and Consuls, and those in which a State shall be Party, the supreme Court shall have original Jurisdiction. In all the other Cases before mentioned, the supreme Court shall have appellate Jurisdiction, both as to Law and Fact, with such Exceptions, and under such Regulations as the Congress shall make.

The Trial of all Crimes, except in Cases of Impeachment, shall be by Jury; and such Trial shall be held in the State where the said Crimes shall have been committed; but when not committed within any State, the Trial shall be at such Place or Places as the Congress may by Law have directed.

Section 3. Treason against the United States, shall consist only in levying War against them, or in adhering to their Enemies, giving them Aid and Comfort. No Person shall be convicted of Treason unless on the Testimony of two Witnesses to the same overt Act, or on Confession in open Court.

The Congress shall have power to declare the punishment of Treason, but no Attainder of Treason shall work Corruption of Blood, or Forfeiture except during the Life of the Person attainted.

Article Four

SECTION 1. FULL FAITH AND CREDIT shall be given in each State to the public Acts, Records, and judicial Proceedings of every other State. And the Congress may by general Laws prescribe the Manner in which such Acts, Records, and Proceedings shall be proved, and the Effect thereof.

Section 2. The Citizens of each State shall be entitled to all Privileges and Immunities of Citizens in the several States.

A Person charged in any State with Treason, Felony, or other Crime, who shall flee from Justice, and be found in another State, shall on Demand of the executive Authority of the State from which he fled, be delivered up, to be removed to the State having Jurisdiction of the Crime.

No person held to Service or Labor in one State, under the Laws thereof, escaping into another, shall, in Consequence of any Law or Regulation therein, be discharged from such Service or Labor, But shall be delivered up on Claim of the Party to whom such Service or Labor may be due.

Section 3. New States may be admitted by the Congress into this Union; but no new States shall be formed or erected within the Jurisdiction of any other State; nor any State be formed by the Junction of two or more States, or Parts of States, without the Consent of the Legislatures of the States concerned as well as of the Congress.

The Congress shall have Power to dispose of and make all needful Rules and Regulations respecting the Territory or other Property belonging to the United States; and nothing in this Constitution shall be so construed as to Prejudice any Claims of the United States, or of any particular State.

Section 4. The United States shall guarantee to every State in this Union a Republican Form of Government, and shall protect each of them against Invasion; and on Application of the Legislature, or of the Executive (when the Legislature cannot be convened) against domestic Violence.

Article Five

THE CONGRESS, WHENEVER TWO THIRDS of both Houses shall deem it necessary, shall propose Amendments to this Constitution, or, on the Application of the Legislatures of two thirds of the several States, shall call a Convention for proposing Amendments, which, in either Case, shall be valid to all Intents and Purposes, as Part of this Constitution, when ratified by the Legislatures of three fourths of the several States, or by Conventions in three fourths thereof, as the one or the other Mode of Ratification may be proposed by the Congress; Provided that no Amendment which may be made prior to the Year one thousand eight hundred and eight shall in any Manner affect the first and fourth Clauses in the ninth Section of the first Article; and that no State, without its Consent, shall be deprived of it's equal Suffrage in the Senate.

Article Six

ALL DEBTS CONTRACTED AND ENGAGEMENTS entered into, before the Adoption of this Constitution, shall be as valid against the United States under this Constitution, as under the Confederation.

This Constitution, and the Laws of the United States which shall be made in Pursuance thereof; and all Treaties made, or which shall be made, under the Authority of the United States, shall be the supreme Law of the Land; and the Judges in every State shall be bound thereby, any Thing in the Constitution or Laws of any State to the Contrary notwithstanding.

The Senators and Representatives before mentioned, and the Members of the several State Legislatures, and all executive and judicial Officers, both of the United States and of the several

States, shall be bound by Oath or Affirmation, to support this Constitution; but no religious Test shall ever be required as a Qualification to any Office or public Trust under the United States

Article Seven

THE RATIFICATION OF THE CONVENTIONS of nine States, shall be sufficient for the Establishment of this Constitution between the States so ratifying the Same.

Done in Convention by the Unanimous Consent of the States present the Seventeenth Day of September in the Year of our Lord one thousand seven hundred and eighty seven and of the Independence of the United States of America the Twelfth In Witness whereof We have hereunto subscribed our Names,

> GO. WASHINGTON—
> Presid. and deputy from Virginia
>
> New Hampshire
>
> John Langdon
> Nicholas Gilman
>
> Massachusetts
>
> Nathaniel Gorham
> Rufus King
>
> Connecticut
>
> Wm. Saml. Johnson
> Roger Sherman
>
> New York
>
> Alexander Hamilton

New Jersey

Wil: Livingston
David Brearley
Wm. Paterson
Jona: Dayton

Pennsylvania

B Franklin
Thomas Mifflin
Robt Morris
Geo. Clymer
Thos FitzSimons
Jared Ingersoll
James Wilson
Gouv Morris

Delaware

Geo: Read
Gunning Bedford jun
John Dickinson
Richard Bassett
Jaco: Broom

Maryland

James Mchenry
Dan of St Thos. Jenifer
Danl Carroll

Virginia

John Blair—
James Madison Jr.

North Carolina

Wm. Blount
Rich'd Dobbs Spaight
Hu Williamson

South Carolina

J. Rutledge
Charles Cotesworth Pinckney
Charles Pinckney
Pierce Butler

Georgia

William Few
Abr Baldwin

Attest:
William Jackson, Secretary

The United States Bill of Rights

I

Congress shall make no law respecting an establishment of religion, or prohibiting the free exercise thereof; or abridging the freedom of speech, or of the press, or the right of the people peaceably to assemble, and to petition the Government for a redress of grievances.

II

A well-regulated militia, being necessary to the security of a free State, the right of the people to keep and bear arms, shall not be infringed.

III

No soldier shall, in time of peace be quartered in any house, without the consent of the owner, nor in time of war, but in a manner to be prescribed by law.

IV

The right of the people to be secure in their persons, houses, papers, and effects, against unreasonable searches and seizures, shall not be violated, and no Warrants shall issue, but upon probable cause, supported by oath or affirmation, and particularly describing the place to be searched, and the persons or things to be seized.

V

No person shall be held to answer for a capital, or otherwise infamous crime, unless on a presentment or indictment of a Grand Jury, except in cases arising in the land or naval forces, or in the Militia, when in actual service in time of War or public danger; nor shall any person be subject for the same offense to be twice put in jeopardy of life or limb; nor shall be compelled in any criminal case to be a witness against himself, nor be deprived of life, liberty, or property, without due process of law; nor shall private property be taken for public use without just compensation.

VI

IN ALL CRIMINAL PROSECUTIONS, THE accused shall enjoy the right to a speedy and public trial, by an impartial jury of the State and district wherein the crime shall have been committed, which district shall have been previously ascertained by law, and to be informed of the nature and cause of the accusation; to be confronted with the witnesses against him; to have compulsory process for obtaining witnesses in his favor, and to have the assistance of counsel for his defense.

VII

IN SUITS AT COMMON LAW, where the value in controversy shall exceed twenty dollars, the right of trial by jury shall be preserved, and no fact tried by a jury shall be otherwise re-examined in any court of the United States, than according to the rules of the common law.

VIII

EXCESSIVE BAIL SHALL NOT BE required nor excessive fines imposed, nor cruel and unusual punishments inflicted.

IX

THE ENUMERATION IN THE CONSTITUTION, of certain rights, shall not be construed to deny or disparage others retained by the people.

X

THE POWERS NOT DELEGATED TO the United States by the Constitution, nor prohibited by it to the States, are reserved to the States respectively, or to the people.

The Indian Removal Act of 1830

An Act to provide for an exchange of lands with the Indians residing in any of the states or territories, and for their removal west of the river Mississippi.

Be it enacted by the Senate and House of Representatives of the United States of America, in Congress assembled, That it shall and may be lawful for the President of the United States to cause so much of any territory belonging to the United States, west of the river Mississippi, not included in any state or organized territory, and to which the Indian title has been extinguished, as he may judge necessary, to be divided into a suitable number of districts, for the reception of such tribes or nations of Indians as may choose to exchange the lands where they now reside, and remove there; and to cause each of said districts to be so described by natural or artificial marks, as to be easily distinguished from every other.

Sec. 2. *And be it further enacted*, That it shall and may be lawful for the President to exchange any or all of such districts, so to be laid off and described, with any tribe or nation of Indians now residing within the limits of any of the states or territories, and with which the United States have existing treaties, for the whole or any part or portion of the territory claimed and occupied by such tribe or nation, within the bounds of anyone or more of the states or territories, where the land claimed and occupied by the Indians, is owned by the United States, or the United States are bound to the state within which it lies to extinguish the Indian claim thereto.

Sec. 3. *And be it further enacted*, That in the making of any such exchange or exchanges, it shall and may be lawful for the President solemnly to assure the tribe or nation with which the exchange is made, that the United States will forever secure and guaranty to them, and their heirs or successors, the country so exchanged with them; and if they prefer it, that the United States will cause a patent or grant to be made and executed to them for the same: *Provided always*, That such lands shall revert to the United States, if the Indians become extinct, or abandon the same.

Sec. 4 And be it further enacted, That if, upon any of the lands now occupied by the Indians, and to be exchanged for, there should be such improvements as add value to the land claimed by any individual or individuals of such tribes or nations, it shall and may be lawful for the President to cause such value to be ascertained by appraisement or otherwise, and to cause such ascertained value to be paid to the person or persons rightfully claiming such improvements. And upon the payment of such valuation, the improvements so valued and paid for, shall pass to the United States, and possession shall not afterwards be permitted to any of the same tribe.

Sec. 5 And be it further enacted, That upon the making of any such exchange as is contemplated by this act, it shall and may be lawful for the President to cause such aid and assistance to be furnished to the emigrants as may be necessary and proper to enable them to remove to, and settle in, the country for which they may have exchanged; and also, to give them such aid and assistance as may be necessary for their support and subsistence for the first year after their removal.

Sec. 6 And be it further enacted, That it shall and may be lawful for the President to cause such tribe or nation to be protected, at their new residence, against all interruption or disturbance from any other tribe or nation of Indians, or from any other person or persons whatever.

Sec. 7 And be it further enacted, That it shall and may be lawful for the President to have the same superintendence and care over any tribe or nation in the country to which they may remove, as contemplated by this act, that he is now authorized to have over them at their present places of residence: Provided, That nothing in this act contained shall be construed as authorizing or directing the violation of any existing treaty between the United States and any of the Indian tribes.

Sec. 8 And be it further enacted, That for the purpose of giving effect to the provisions of this act, the sum of five hundred thousand dollars is hereby appropriated, to be paid out of any money in the treasury, not otherwise appropriated.

Approved, May 28, 1830.

The Indians Appropriations Act

1851

An Act making Appropriations for the Payment of Revolutionary and other Pensions of the United States, for the Year ending in the thirtieth of June, one thousand eight hundred and fifty-two.

Be it enacted by the Senate and House of Representatives of the United States of America in Congress assembled, That the following sums be, and they are hereby, appropriated out of any money in the treasury not otherwise appropriated, for the purpose of paying the current and contingent expenses of the Indian department, and fulfilling treaty stipulations with the various Indian tribes.

For the current and contingent expenses of the Indian department, viz.

For the pay of superintendents of Indian affairs, and the several Superintend Indian agents, as provided by the acts of June thirtieth, eighteen hundred and thirty-four, and March third, eighteen hundred and thirty-seven, and of June twenty-seventh, eighteen hundred and forty-six, and June fifth, eighteen hundred and fifty, and of September twenty-eighth, eighteen hundred and fifty, thirty-four thousand dollars.

For the pay of sub-Indian agents, authorized by the act of June thirtieth, eighteen hundred and thirty-four, thirteen thousand five hundred dollars.

For pay of interpreters, authorized by the same act, sixteen thousand late five hundred dollars.

For pay of clerk to superintendent at St. Louis, authorized by the act of June twenty-seventh, eighteen hundred and forty-six, one thousand two hundred dollars.

For pay of clerk to acting superintendent of the Western Territory, by the same act, one thousand dollars.

For buildings at agencies and repairs thereof, two thousand dollars.

For presents to Indians, five thousand dollars.

For provisions for Indians, eleven thousand eight hundred dollars.

For contingencies of the Indian department, thirty-six thousand five hundred dollars.

To the Christian Indians.—For permanent annuity, stipulated in the acts of May twenty-sixth, eighteen hundred and twenty-four, and May twentieth, eighteen hundred and twenty-six, four hundred dollars.

To the Chippewas of Saganaw.—For permanent annuity, stipulated in the fourth article of the treaty of third August, seventeen hundred and ninety-five, one thousand dollars.

For permanent annuity, stipulated in the second article of the treaty of seventeenth of November, eighteen hundred and seven, eight hundred dollars.

For permanent annuity, stipulated in the fourth article of the treaty of twenty-fourth September, eighteen hundred and nineteen, one thousand dollars.

For permanent provision for the support of blacksmiths, and for farming utensils and cattle, and the employment of persons to aid them in agriculture, stipulated in the eighth article of the treaty of twenty-fourth September, eighteen hundred and nineteen, and the seventh article of the treaty of fourteenth January, eighteen hundred and thirty-seven, two thousand dollars.

For education, during the pleasure of Congress, stipulated in the sixth article of the treaty of fifth August, eighteen hundred and twenty-six, one thousand dollars.

To the Chippewas, Menomones, Winnebagoes, and New York Indians.—For education, during the pleasure of Congress, stipulated in the fifth article of the treaty of eleventh August, eighteen hundred and twenty-seven, one thousand five hundred dollars.

To the Chippewas of Lake Superior and Mississippi.—For fifteenth of twenty instalments, in money, stipulated in the second article of the treaty of twenty-ninth July, eighteen hundred and thirty-seven, nine thousand five hundred dollars.

For fifteenth of twenty instalments in goods, stipulated in the second article of the treaty of twenty-ninth July, eighteen hundred and thirty-seven, nineteen thousand dollars.

For fifteenth of twenty instalments for the establishment of three smith's shops, supporting three smiths, and furnishing iron and steel, stipulated in the second article of the treaty of twenty-ninth July, eighteen hundred and thirty-seven, three thousand dollars.

For fifteenth of twenty instalments for the support of farmers, purchase of implements, grain, or seed, and to carry on their agricultural pursuits, stipulated in the second article of the treaty of the twenty ninth of July, eighteen hundred and thirty-seven, one thousand dollars.

For fifteenth of twenty instalments for the purchase of tobacco, stipulated in the second article of the treaty of twenty ninth July, eighteen hundred and thirty-seven, five hundred dollars.

For fifteenth of twenty instalments for the purchase of provisions, stipulated in the second article of the treaty of twenty-ninth July, eighteen hundred and thirty-seven, two thousand dollars.

For tenth of twenty-five instalments, in money, stipulated in the fourth article of the treaty of fourth October, eighteen hundred and forty-two, twelve thousand five hundred dollars.

For tenth of twenty-five instalments, in goods, stipulated in the fourth article of the treaty of fourth October, eighteen hundred and forty-two, ten thousand five hundred dollars.

For tenth of twenty-five instalments for the support of two smith's shops, including pay of smiths and assistants, and furnishing iron and steel, stipulated in the fourth article of the treaty of fourth October eighteen hundred and forty-two, two thousand dollars.

For tenth of twenty-five instalments for the pay of two farmers, stipulated in the fourth article of the treaty of fourth October, eighteen hundred and forty-two, one thousand dollars.

For tenth of twenty-five instalments for the pay of two carpenters, stipulated in the fourth article of the treaty of fourth October, eighteen hundred and forty-two, one thousand two hundred dollars.

For tenth of twenty-five instalments for the support of schools, stipulated in the fourth article of the treaty of fourth October, eighteen hundred and forty-two, two thousand dollars.

For tenth of twenty-five instalments for the purchase of provisions and tobacco, stipulated in the fourth article of the treaty of fourth October, eighteen hundred and forty-two, two thousand dollars.

For fifth of five instalments in goods payable to the Pillager Band, stipulated in the fourth article of the treaty of twenty-first August, eighteen hundred and forty-seven, three thousand six hundred dollars.

For fifth of forty-six instalments to be paid to the Chippewes of Mississippi, stipulated in the third article of the treaty of second August, eighteen hundred and forty-seven, one thousand dollars.

To the Chickasaws.—For permanent annuity, stipulated in the act of the twenty-fifth February, seventeen hundred and ninety-nine, three thousand dollars.

For permanent annuity, stipulated in the thirteenth article of the treaty of eighteenth October, eighteen hundred and twenty, six hundred dollars.

For life annuity to chief Bob Cole, stipulated in the tenth article of the treaty of twentieth January, eighteen hundred and twenty-five, one hundred and fifty dollars.

For permanent annuity for education, stipulated in the second article of the treaty of twentieth January, eighteen hundred and twenty-five, six thousand dollars.

For annuity to three district chiefs, stipulated in the fifteenth article of the treaty of twenty-seventh September, eighteen hundred and thirty, seven hundred and fifty dollars.

For life annuity to one Wayne warrior, stipulated in the twenty-first article of the treaty of twenty-seventh September, eighteen hundred and thirty, twenty-five dollars.

For permanent provision for blacksmiths, stipulated in the sixth article of the treaty of eighteenth October, eighteen hundred and twenty, and ninth article of the treaty of twentieth January, eighteen hundred and twenty-five, six hundred dollars.

For iron and steel, etc., for shop, stipulated in the ninth article of the treaty of twentieth January, eighteen hundred and twenty-five, three hundred and twenty dollars.

To the Creeks.—For permanent annuity, stipulated in the fourth article of the treaty of seventh August, seventeen hundred and ninety, one thousand five hundred dollars.

For permanent annuity, stipulated in the second article of the treaty sixteenth June, eighteen hundred and two, three thousand dollars.

For permanent annuity, stipulated in the fourth article of the treaty twenty-fourth January, eighteen hundred and twenty-six, twenty thousand dollars.

For twentieth, of twenty instalments in money, stipulated in the eighth article of the treaty of twenty-fourth March, eighteen hundred and thirty-two, ten thousand dollars.

For permanent provision for blacksmith and assistant, stipulated in the eighth article of the treaty of twenty-fourth January, eighteen hundred and twenty-six, eight hundred and forty dollars.

For iron and steel for shop, two hundred and seventy dollars.

For fifteenth of twenty instalments for the pay of two blacksmiths and assistants, stipulated in the thirteenth article of the treaty of twenty-fourth March, eighteen hundred and thirty-two, one thousand six hundred and eighty dollars.

For iron, steel, etc., for shops, five hundred and forty dollars.

For permanent provision for the pay of a wheelwright, stipulated in the eighth article of the treaty of twenty-fourth January, eighteen hundred and twenty-six, six hundred dollars.

For twenty-first of thirty-three instalments for education, stipulated in the thirteenth article of the treaty of twenty-fourth March, eighteen hundred and thirty-two, and fourth article of the treaty of fourth January, eighteen hundred and forty-five, three thousand dollars.

For interest on three hundred and fifty thousand dollars, at five per centum, stipulated in the third article of the treaty of twenty-third November, eighteen hundred and thirty-eight, seventeen thousand five hundred dollars.

For eighth of twenty instalments for education, stipulated in the fourth article of the treaty of the fourth January, eighteen hundred and forty-five, three thousand dollars.

For blacksmith and assistant, during the pleasure of the President, stipulated in the fifth article of the treaty of fourteenth February, eighteen hundred and thirty-three, eight hundred and forty dollars.

For iron, steel, and coal, during the pleasure of the President, stipulated in the fifth article of the treaty of fourteenth February, eighteen hundred and thirty-three, two hundred and seventy dollars.

For wagon maker, during the pleasure of the President, stipulated in the fifth article of the treaty of fourteenth February, eighteen hundred and thirty-three, six hundred dollars.

For agricultural implements, during the pleasure of the President, stipulated in the eighth article of the treaty of twenty-fourth January, eighteen hundred and twenty-six, two thousand dollars.

For education, during the pleasure of the President, stipulated in the fifth article of the treaty of fourteenth February, eighteen hundred and thirty-three, one thousand dollars.

To the Delawares.—For permanent annuity, stipulated in the fourth article of the treaty of third August, seventeen hundred and ninety-five, one thousand dollars.

For permanent annuity, stipulated in the third article of the treaty of thirtieth September, eighteen hundred and nine, five hundred dollars.

For permanent annuity, stipulated in the fifth article of the treaty of third October, eighteen hundred and eighteen, four thousand dollars.

For permanent annuity, stipulated in the supplemental treaty of twenty-fourth September, eighteen hundred and twenty-nine, one thousand dollars.

For life annuity to chiefs, stipulated in the private article of supplemental treaty of twenty-fourth September, eighteen hundred and twenty nine, to treaty of third October, eighteen hundred and eighteen, two hundred dollars.

For life annuity to chiefs, stipulated in the supplemental article to treaty of twenty-sixth October, eighteen hundred and thirty-two, two hundred dollars.

For permanent provision for the purchase of salt, stipulated in the third article of the treaty of seventh June, eighteen hundred and three, one hundred dollars.

For permanent provision for blacksmith and assistant, stipulated in the sixth article of the treaty of third October, eighteen hundred and eighteen, seven hundred and twenty dollars.

For iron and steel for shop, two hundred and twenty dollars.

For interest on forty-six thousand and eighty dollars, at five per centum, being the value of thirty-six sections of land, set apart by treaty of eighteen hundred and twenty-nine, for education, stipulated in resolution of the Senate of nineteenth January, eighteen hundred and thirty-eight, two thousand three hundred and four dollars.

To the Florida Indians, or Seminoles.—For twenty-ninth of thirty instalments for blacksmith's establishment, stipulated in the sixth article of the treaty of eighteenth September, eighteen hundred and twenty-three, and fourth article of the treaty of ninth May, eighteen hundred and thirty-two, one thousand dollars.

For eighth of fifteen instalments, in goods, stipulated in the sixth article of the treaty of fourth January, eighteen hundred and forty-five, two thousand dollars.

For eighth of fifteen instalments, in money, stipulated in the fourth article of the treaty of fourth January, eighteen hundred and forty-five, three thousand dollars.

To the Iowas.—For interest on one hundred and fifty-seven thousand five hundred dollars, at five per centum, stipulated in the second article of the treaty of nineteenth October, eighteen hundred and thirty eight, seven thousand eight hundred and seventy-five dollars

To the Kickapoos.—For eighteenth of nineteen instalments, as annuity, stipulated in the fourth article of the treaty of twenty-fourth October, eighteen hundred and thirty-two, five thousand dollars

To the Kansas.—For interest on two hundred thousand dollars, at five per centum, stipulated in the second article of the treaty of fourteenth January, eighteen hundred and forty-six, ten thousand dollars.

To the Miamies.—For permanent annuity, stipulated in the fourth article of the treaty of twenty-third October, eighteen hundred and twenty-six, twenty-five thousand dollars.

For permanent provision for blacksmith and assistant, stipulated in the fifth article of the treaty of sixth October, eighteen hundred and seven hundred and twenty dollars.

For iron and steel for shop, two hundred and twenty dollars.

For permanent provision for the purchase of one thousand pounds of tobacco, two thousand pounds of iron, and one thousand pounds of steel, stipulated in the fourth article of the treaty of twenty-third October, eighteen hundred and twenty-six, seven hundred and seventy dollars.

For permanent provision for pay of miller, in lien of gunsmith, stipulated in the fifth article of the treaty of the sixth October, eighteen hundred and eighteen, and fifth article of the treaty of second (28d) October, eighteen hundred and thirty-four, six hundred dollars.

For permanent provision for the purchase of one hundred and sixty bushels of salt, stipulated in the fifth article of the treaty of sixth October, eighteen hundred and eighteen, three hundred and twenty dollars.

For education and support of poor, during the pleasure of Congress, stipulated in the sixth article of treaty of twenty-third October, eighteen hundred and twenty-six, two thousand dollars.

For eleventh of twenty instalments, in money, stipulated in the second article of the treaty of twenty-eighth November, eighteen hundred and forty, twelve thousand five hundred dollars.

For permanent provision for payment in lieu of laborers, stipulated in the sixth article of the treaty of twenty-eighth November, eighteen hundred and forty, two hundred and fifty dollars.

For permanent provision for agricultural assistance, stipulated in the fifth article of the treaty of sixth October, eighteen hundred and eighteen, two hundred dollars.

To the Eel Rivers, (Miamies.)—For permanent annuity, stipulated Set Rivers, in the fourth article of the treaty of third August, seventeen hundred and ninety-five, five hundred dollars.

For permanent annuity, stipulated in the third article of the treaty of twenty-first August, eighteen hundred and five, two hundred and fifty dollars.

For permanent annuity, stipulated in the third article, and separate article, of the treaty of the thirtieth September, eighteen hundred and nine, three hundred and fifty dollars: *Provided*, That the several sums proviso. hereby appropriated to the Eel Rivers (*Miamies*) shall not be paid until satisfactory proof is obtained, by the commissioner of Indian affairs, of the existence of such band of Indians, and shall then be paid to such band only: *And provided farther*, That if said commissioner obtains satisfactory proof that the annuities, or any part thereof, due said Eel Rivers, have heretofore, erroneously or otherwise, been paid to any other band or nation of Indians, such sums thus paid shall be reimbursed to said Eel Rivers, if their existence is established, in such instalments as the commissioner may direct, out of the annuities of the nation or band to which they were thus paid.

To the Menomonees.—For sixteenth of twenty instalments as annuity, stipulated in the second article of the treaty of third September, eighteen hundred and thirty-six, twenty thousand dollars.

For sixteenth of twenty instalments for two blacksmiths and assistants, stipulated in the second article of the treaty of third September, eighteen hundred and thirty-six, one thousand four hundred and forty dollars.

For sixteenth of twenty instalments for iron, steel, etc., for shops, stipulated in the second article of the treaty of third September, eighteen hundred and thirty-six, four hundred and forty dollars.

For sixteenth of twenty instalments for the purchase of provisions, stipulated in the second article of the treaty of third September, eighteen hundred and thirty-six, three thousand dollars.

For sixteenth of twenty instalments for the purchase of two thousand pounds of tobacco, stipulated in the second article of the treaty of third September, eighteen hundred and thirty-six, three hundred dollars.

For sixteenth of twenty instalments for farming utensils and cattle; stipulated in the second article of the treaty of third September, eighteen hundred and thirty-six, five hundred dollars.

For sixteenth of twenty instalments for thirty barrels of salt, stipulated in the second article of the treaty of third September, eighteen hundred and thirty-six, one hundred and fifty dollars.

To the Omahas.—For blacksmith and assistant, during the pleasure of the President, stipulated in the fourth article of the treaty of fifteenth July, eighteen hundred and thirty, seven hundred and twenty dollars.

For iron and steel, etc., for shops, during the pleasure of the President, two hundred and twenty dollars.

For agricultural implements, during the pleasure of the President, stipulated in the fourth article of the treaty of fifteenth July, eighteen hundred and thirty, five hundred dollars.

To the Ottoes and the Missourias.—For education, daring the pleasure of the President, stipulated in the fourth article of the treaty of twenty-first September, eighteen hundred and thirty-three, five hundred dollars.

For pay of farmer, during the pleasure of the President, stipulated in the fifth article of the treaty of twenty-first September, eighteen hundred and thirty-three, six hundred dollars.

For blacksmith and assistant, during the pleasure of the President, stipulated in the fourth article of the treaty of fifteenth July, eighteen hundred and thirty, seven hundred and twenty dollars.

For iron and steel for shop, during the pleasure of the President, two hundred and twenty dollars.

To the Ottowas.—For permanent annuity, stipulated in the fourth article of treaty of the third August, seventeen hundred and ninety-five, one thousand dollars.

For permanent annuity, stipulated in the second article of the treaty of seventeenth November, eighteen hundred and seven, eight hundred dollars.

For permanent annuity, stipulated in the fourth article of the treaty of seventeenth September, eighteen hundred and eighteen, one thousand five hundred dollars.

For permanent annuity, stipulated in the fourth article of the treaty of twenty-ninth August, eighteen hundred and twenty-one, one thousand dollars.

To the Ottawas and Chippewas.—For seventeenth of twenty instalments, stipulated in the fourth article of the treaty of twenty-eighth March, eighteen hundred and thirty-six, thirty thousand dollars.

For interest, to be paid as annuity on two hundred thousand dollars, stipulated in the resolution of the Senate of the twenty-seventh May, eighteen hundred and thirty-six, twelve thousand dollars.

For education, for twenty years, and during the pleasure of Congress, stipulated in the fourth article of the treaty of twenty-eighth arch, eighteen hundred and thirty-six, five thousand dollars.

For missions, for twenty years, and during the pleasure of Congress, stipulated in the fourth article of the treaty of twenty-eighth March, eighteen hundred and thirty-six, three thousand dollars.

For vaccine matter, medicines, and pay of physicians, so long as the Indians remain on their reservations, stipulated in the fourth article of the treaty of twenty-eighth March, eighteen hundred and thirty-six, three hundred dollars.

For seventeenth of twenty instalments for the purchase of provisions, stipulated in the fourth article of the treaty of twenty-eighth March, eighteen hundred and thirty-six, two thousand dollars.

For seventeenth of twenty instalments for the purchase of six thousand five hundred pounds of tobacco, stipulated in. the fourth article of the treaty of twenty-eight March, eighteen hundred and thirty-nix, five hundred dollars.

For seventeenth of twenty instalments for the purchase of one hundred barrels of salt, stipulated in the fourth article of the treaty of twenty-eighth March, eighteen hundred and thirty-six, two hundred dollars.

For seventeenth of twenty instalments, for the purchase of five hundred fish barrels, stipulated in the fourth article of the treaty of twenty-eighth March, eighteen hundred and thirty-nix, four hundred dollars.

For three blacksmiths and assistants, for twenty years, and during the pleasure of Congress, stipulated in the seventh article of the treaty of twenty-eight March, eighteen hundred and thirty-six, two thousand one hundred and sixty dollars.

For iron, steel, etc., for shops, for twenty years, and during the pleasure of Congress, stipulated in the seventh article of the treaty of twenty-eighth March, eighteen hundred and thirty-six, six hundred and sixty-dollars.

For gunsmith at Mackinac, for twenty years, and during the pleasure of Congress, stipulated in the seventh article of the treaty of twenty-eighth March, eighteen hundred and thirty-six, six hundred dollars.

For iron, steel, etc., for shop, for twenty years, and during the pleasure of Congress, stipulated in the seventh article of the treaty of twenty-eighth March, eighteen hundred and thirty-six, two hundred and twenty dollars.

For two farmers and assistants, during the pleasure of the President, stipulated in the seventh article of the treaty of twenty-eighth March, eighteen hundred and thirty-six, one thousand six hundred dollars.

For two mechanics, during the pleasure of the President, stipulated in the seventh article of the treaty of twenty-eighth March, eighteen hundred and thirty-six, one thousand two hundred dollars.

The Osages.—For interest on sixty-nine thousand one hundred and twenty dollars, at five per centum, being the valuation of fifty-four sections of land set apart by treaty of the second June, eighteen hundred and twenty-five, for educational purposes, per resolution of the Senate nineteenth January, eighteen hundred and thirty-eight three thousand four hundred and fifty-six dollars

For fourteenth of, twenty instalments, as annuity, stipulated in the second article of the treaty of the eleventh January, eighteen hundred and thirty-nine, twenty thousand dollars.

For fourteenth of twenty instalments for two smiths' establishments, stipulated in the second article of the treaty of the eleventh January, eighteen hundred and thirty-nine, two thousand dollars.

For fourteenth of fifteen instalments for pay of two millers, stipulated in the second article of the treaty of eleventh January, eighteen hundred and thirty-nine, one thousand two hundred dollars.

To the Piankeshaws.—For permanent annuity, stipulated in the fourth article of the treaty of third August, seventeen hundred and ninety-five hundred dollars.

For permanent annuity, stipulated in the third article of the treaty of the thirtieth December, eighteen hundred and five, three hundred dollars.

To the Pawnees.—For agricultural implements, during the pleasure of the President, stipulated in the fourth article of the treaty of the ninth October, eighteen hundred and thirty-three, one thousand dollars.

To the Potawatamies of Huron.—For permanent annuity, stipulated in the second article of the treaty of the seventeenth November, of eighteen hundred and seven, four hundred dollars

To the Potawatamies.—For permanent annuity, stipulated in the fourth article of the treaty of third August, seventeen hundred and ninety-five, one thousand dollars.

For permanent annuity, stipulated in the third article of the treaty of thirtieth September, eighteen hundred and nine, five hundred dollars.

For permanent annuity, stipulated in the third article of the treaty of second October, eighteen hundred and eighteen, two thousand five hundred dollars.

For permanent annuity, stipulated in the second article of the treaty of twentieth September, eighteen hundred and twenty-eight, two thousand dollars.

For life annuity to chief, stipulated in the second article of the treaty of the twentieth September, eighteen hundred and twenty-eight, one hundred dollars.

For permanent annuity, stipulated in the second article of the treaty of twenty-ninth July, eighteen hundred and twenty-nine, sixteen thousand dollars.

For nineteenth of twenty instalments, as annuity, stipulated in the third article of the treaty of twentieth of October, eighteen hundred and thirty-two, fifteen thousand dollars.

For life annuity to chiefs, stipulated in the third article of the treaty of twentieth October, eighteen hundred and thirty-two, four hundred dollars.

For nineteenth of twenty instalments, as annuity, stipulated in the third article of the treaty of twenty-six October, eighteen hundred and thirty-two, twenty thousand dollars.

For seventeenth of twenty instalments, as annuity, stipulated in the third article of the treaty of the twenty-six September, eighteen hundred and thirty-three, fourteen thousand dollars.

For life annuity to chiefs, stipulated in the third article of the treaty of twenty-sixth of September, eighteen hundred and thirty-three, seven hundred dollars.

For seventeenth of twenty instalments, as annuity, stipulated in the second supplemental article of the treaty of twenty-six-September, eighteen hundred grid thirty-three, two thousand dollars.

For permanent provision for the purchase of salt, stipulated in the third article of the treaty of seventh June, eighteen hundred and three, one hundred and forty dollars.

For permanent provision for the purchase of one hundred and sixty bushels of salt, stipulated in the third article of the treaty of sixteenth October, eighteen hundred and twenty-six, three hundred and twenty dollars.

For education, during the pleasure of Congress, stipulated in the third article of the treaty of the sixteenth October, eighteen hundred and twenty-six, two thousand dollars.

For permanent provision for blacksmith and assistant, stipulated in the third article of the treaty of sixteenth October, eighteen hundred and twenty-six, seven hundred and twenty dollars.

For permanent provision for iron, steel, etc., for shop, stipulated in the third article of the treaty of sixteenth October, eighteen hundred and twenty-six, two hundred and twenty dollars.

For education, during the pleasure of Congress, stipulated in the second article of the treaty of the twentieth September, eighteen hundred and twenty-eight, one thousand dollars.

For permanent provision for the payment in money, in lieu of two thousand pounds of tobacco, fifteen hundred pounds of iron, and three hundred and fifty pounds of steel, stipulated in the second article of the treaty of twentieth September, eighteen hundred and twenty-eight, and the tenth article of the treaty of fifth June, eighteen hundred and forty-six, three hundred dollars.

For permanent provision for blacksmith and assistant, stipulated in the second article of the treaty of twentieth September, eighteen hundred and twenty-eight, seven hundred and twenty dollars.

For permanent provision for iron, steel, etc., for shop, stipulated in the second article of the treaty of twentieth September, eighteen hundred and twenty-eight, two hundred and twenty dollars.

For permanent provision for blacksmith and assistant, stipulated in the second article of the treaty of twenty-ninth July, eighteen hundred and twenty-nine, seven hundred and twenty dollars.

For permanent provision for iron, steel, etc., for shop, stipulated in the second article of the treaty of twenty-ninth July, eighteen hundred and twenty-nine, two hundred and twenty dollars.

For permanent provision for the purchase of fifty barrels of salt, stipulated in the second article of the treaty of the twenty-ninth of July, eighteen hundred and twenty-nine, two hundred and fifty dollars.

For education, during the pleasure of Congress, stipulated in the fourth article of the treaty of the twenty-seventh October, eighteen hundred and thirty-two, two thousand dollars.

For interest on six hundred and forty-three thousand dollars, at five per centum, stipulated in the seventh article of the treaty of the fifth June, eighteen hundred and forty-six, thirty-two thousand one hundred and fifty dollars.

To the Quapaws.—For nineteenth of twenty instalments, as annuity, stipulated in the fourth article of the treaty of thirteenth May, eighteen hundred and thirty-three, two thousand dollars.

For education, during the pleasure of the President, stipulated in the third article of the treaty of thirteenth May, eighteen hundred and thirty three, one thousand dollars.

For blacksmith and assistant, during the pleasure of the President, stipulated in the third article of the treaty of thirteenth May, eighteen hundred and thirty-three, eight hundred and forty dollars.

For iron, steel, etc., for shop, during the pleasure of the President, stipulated in the third article of the treaty of thirteenth May, eighteen hundred and thirty-three, two hundred and twenty dollars.

For pay of farmer, during the pleasure of the President, stipulated in the third article of the treaty of thirteenth May, eighteen hundred and thirty-three, six hundred dollars.

To the Six Nations of New York.—For permanent annuity, stipulated in the sixth article of the treaty of eleventh November, seventeen hundred and ninety-four, four thousand five hundred dollars.

To the Senecas of New York.—For permanent annuity, in lieu of interest on stock, per act of the nineteenth February, eighteen Now hundred and thirty-one, six thousand dollars.

For interest, in lieu of investment, on seventy-five thousand dollars, at five per centum, per act of the twenty-seventh June, eighteen hundred and forty-six, three thousand seven hundred and fifty dollars.

To the Stockbridges.—For interest on sixteen thousand five hundred dollars at five per centum, stipulated in the ninth article of the treaty of the twenty-fourth November, eighteen hundred and forty-eight, eight hundred and twenty-five dollars.

To the Sioux of Mississippi.—For interest on three hundred thousand dollars, at five per centum, stipulated in the second article of the treaty of twenty-ninth September, eighteen hundred and thirty-seven, fifteen thousand dollars, or fifteenth of twenty instalments as annuity, in goods, stipulated in the second article of the treaty of twenty-ninth September, eighteen hundred and thirty-seven, ten thousand dollars.

For fifteenth of twenty instalments for the purchase of medicines, agricultural implements, and stock, and for support of farmers, physicians, and blacksmiths, etc., stipulated in the second article of the treaty of the twenty-ninth September, eighteen, hundred and thirty-seven, eight thousand two hundred and fifty dollars.

For fifteenth of twenty instalments, for the purchase of provisions, stipulated in the second article of the treaty of twenty-ninth September, eighteen hundred and thirty-seven, five thousand five hundred dollars.

To the Sacs and Foxes of Missouri.—For interest on one hundred and fifty-seven thousand four hundred dollars, at five per centum, stipulated in the second article of the treaty of the twenty-first October, eighteen hundred and thirty-seven, seven thousand eight hundred and seventy dollars.

To the Sacs and Foxes of Mississippi.—For permanent annuity, of s stipulated in the third article of the treaty of third November, eighteen hundred and four, one thousand dollars.

For twentieth of thirty instalments as annuity, stipulated in the third article of the treaty of twenty-first September, eighteen hundred and thirty-two, twenty thousand dollars.

For twentieth of thirty instalments for gunsmith, stipulated in the fourth article of the treaty of twenty-first September, eighteen hundred and thirty-two, six hundred dollars.

For twentieth of thirty instalments for iron, steel, etc., for shop, stipulated in the fourth article of the treaty of twenty-first September, eighteen hundred and thirty two, two hundred and twenty dollars.

For twentieth of thirty instalments for blacksmith and assistant, stipulated in the fourth article of the treaty of twenty-first September, eighteen hundred and-thirty-two, eight hundred and forty dollars.

For twentieth of thirty instalments for iron, steel, etc., for shop, stipulated in the fourth article of the treaty of twenty-first September, eighteen hundred and thirty-two, two hundred and twenty dollars.

For twentieth of thirty instalments for forty barrels of salt, stipulated in the fourth article of the treaty of twenty-first September, eighteen hundred and thirty-two, two hundred dollars.

For twentieth of thirty instalments for forty kegs of tobacco, stipulated in the fourth article of the treaty of twenty-first September, eighteen hundred and thirty-two, six hundred dollars.

For interest on two hundred thousand dollars, at five per centum, stipulated in the second article of the treaty of the twenty-first October, eighteen hundred and thirty-seven, ten thousand dollars.

For interest on eight hundred thousand dollars at five per centum stipulated in the second article of the treaty of the eleventh October, eighteen hundred and forty-two, forty thousand dollars.

To the Shawnees.—For permanent annuity, stipulated in the fourth article of the treaty of third August, seventeen hundred and ninety-five, one thousand dollars.

For permanent annuity, stipulated in the fourth article of the treaty of twenty-ninth September, eighteen hundred and seventeen, two thousand dollars.

For permanent provision for the purchase of salt, stipulated in the third article of the treaty of the seventh June, eighteen-hundred and three, sixty dollars.

For blacksmith and assistant, during the pleasure of the President, stipulated in the fourth article of the treaty of eighth August, eighteen hundred and thirty-one, eight hundred and forty dollars.

For iron, steel, etc., for shop, during the pleasure of the President, stipulated in the fourth article of the treaty of eighth August, eighteen hundred and thirty-one, two hundred and twenty dollars.

To the Sencas and Shawnees.—For permanent annuity, stipulated in the fourth article of the treaty of seventeenth September, eighteen hundred and eighteen, one thousand dollars.

For blacksmith and assistant, during the pleasure of the President, stipulated in the fourth article of the treaty of twentieth July, eighteen hundred and thirty-one, eight hundred and forty dollars.

For iron, steel, etc., for shops, during the pleasure of the President, stipulated in the fourth article of the treaty of twentieth July, eighteen hundred and thirty-one, two hundred and twenty dollars.

To the Senecas.—For permanent annuity stipulated in the fourth article of the treaty of the twenty-ninth September, eighteen hundred and seventeen, five hundred dollars.

For permanent annuity, stipulated in the fourth article of the treaty of the seventeenth September, eighteen hundred and eighteen, five hundred dollars.

For blacksmith and assistant, during the pleasure of the President, stipulated in the fourth article of the treaty of the twenty-eighth February, eighteen hundred and thirty-one, eight hundred and forty dollars.

For iron and steel for shop, during the pleasure of the President, two hundred and twenty dollars.

For pay of miller, during the pleasure of the President, stipulated in the fourth article of the treaty of twenty-eighth February, eighteen hundred and thirty-one, six hundred dollars.

To the Wyandots.—For permanent annuity, stipulated in the third article of the treaty of the seventeenth March, eighteen hundred and forty-two, seventeen thousand five hundred dollars.

For permanent provision for blacksmith and assistant, stipulated in the eighth article of the treaty of the seventeenth March, eighteen hundred and forty-two, seven hundred and twenty dollars.

For permanent provision for iron, steel, etc., for shop, three hundred and seventy dollars.

For permanent provision for education, stipulated in the fourth article of the treaty of the seventeenth March, eighteen hundred and forty-two, five hundred dollars.

To the Winnebagoes.—For twenty-third of thirty instalments, as annuity, stipulated in the second article of the treaty of the first

August, eighteen hundred and twenty-nine, eighteen thousand dollars.

For twentieth of twenty-seven instalments, as annuity, stipulated in the third article of the treaty of the fifteenth September, eighteen hundred and thirty-two, ten thousand dollars.

For twenty-third of thirty instalments for the purchase of fifty barrels of salt, stipulated in the second article of the treaty of the first August, eighteen hundred and twenty-nine, two hundred and fifty dollars.

For twenty-third of thirty instalments for the purchase of three thousand pounds of tobacco, stipulated in the second article of the treaty of the first August, eighteen hundred and twenty-nine, three hundred and fifty dollars.

For twentieth of twenty-seven instalments for the purchase of one thousand five hundred pounds of tobacco, stipulated in the fifth article of the treaty of the fifteenth September, eighteen hundred and thirty-two, one hundred and seventy-five dollars.

For twenty-third of thirty instalments for three blacksmiths and assistants, stipulated in the third article of the treaty of the first August, eighteen hundred and twenty-nine, two thousand one hundred and sixty dollars.

For twenty-third of thirty instalments for iron, steel, etc., for shop, six hundred and sixty dollars.

For twenty-third of thirty instalments for laborers and oxen, stipulated in the third article of the treaty of the first August, eighteen hundred and twenty-nine, three hundred and sixty-five dollars.

For twentieth of twenty-seven instalments for education, stipulated in the fourth article of the treaty of the fifteenth September, eighteen hundred and thirty-two, three thousand dollars.

For twentieth of twenty-seven instalments for six agriculturists, purchase of oxen, ploughs, and other implements, stipulated in the fifth article of the treaty of the fifteenth September, eighteen hundred and thirty-two, two thousand five hundred dollars.

For twentieth of twenty-seven instalments for pay of two physicians, stipulated in the fifth article of the treaty of the fifteenth September, eighteen hundred and thirty-two, four hundred dollars.

For interest on one million one hundred thousand dollars, at five per centum, stipulated in the fourth article of the treaty of the first November, eighteen hundred and thirty-seven, fifty-five thousand dollars.

For interest on eighty-five thousand dollars, at five per centum, stipulated in the fourth article of the treaty of the thirteenth October, eighteen hundred and forty-six, four thousand two hundred and fifty dollars.

To the Weas.—For permanent annuity, stipulated in the fifth article of the treaty of second October, eighteen hundred and eighteen, three thousand dollars.

To defray the expenses of the chiefs of the Oneida Indians in Wisconsin, on a visit to Washington in eighteen hundred and fifty-one, in relation to their treaties with the United States, rendered necessary by the deranged condition of their affairs with the federal government, one thousand dollars.

For arrearages due the first Christian and Orchard parties of Oneida Indians in Wisconsin, under the treaty of seventeen hundred and ninety-six, one thousand seven hundred and sixty-four dollars and eighty cents.

SEC. 2[1]. *And be it further enacted*, That from and after the thirtieth eats of Indian day of June next, all laws or parts of laws now in force, (a) providing for the appointment or, employment of superintendents of Indian affairs, of whatever character, for any of the Indian tribes east of the Rocky Mountains, and north of New Mexico and Texas, shall be, and the same are hereby repealed; and that the President be, and he is hereby, authorized by and with the advice and consent of the Senate, to appoint three superintendents of Indian affairs, for said Indians, who shall receive an annual salary each of two thousand dollars, and whose duty, it shall be to exercise a general superintendance over such tribes of Indians as the President of the United States, or the Secretary of the Department of the Interior may direct,

---

1. Superintendents of Indian affairs east of Rocky Mountains (a).

and to execute and perform all the powers and duties now assigned by law to superintendents of Indian affairs: *Provided*, That the governor of Minnesota shall continue to be, ex officio, superintendent of Indian affairs, for that Territory until the President shall otherwise direct.

SEC. 3.[2] *And be it further enacted*, That hereafter all Indian treaties Indian treaties shall be negotiated by such officers and agents of the Indian department as the President of the United States may designate for that purpose, and no officer or agent so employed shall receive any additional compensation for such service.

SEC. 4[3]. *And be it further enacted*, That in lieu of the twenty-three agents and sub-agents, heretofore employed for the Indians east of the Rocky Mountains, and north of New Mexico and Texas, the President be, and he is hereby, authorized by and with the advice and consent of the Senate, to appoint eleven Indian agents, who shall each receive an annual salary of fifteen hundred dollars; and, also, six other agents, with an annual salary each of one thousand dollars, whose appointments shall take effect from and after the thirtieth day of June next; and the said agents shall execute and perform all the powers and duties now assigned by law to Indian agents.

Sec. 5[4]. *And be it further enacted*, That the President be authorized, by and with the advice and consent of the Senate, to appoint four agents for the Indians in the territory of New Mexico, and one agent for those in the territory of Utah[5], who shall receive an annual salary each of fifteen hundred and fifty dollars, and perform all the duties of agent to such Indians or tribes, as shall be assigned them by the Superintendents of Indian Affairs for these territories respectively, under the direction of the President, or the Secretary of the Department of the Interior.

Sec. 6. *And be it further enacted*, That the superintendents and agents to be appointed under the provisions of this act, before

---

2. Negotiation of Indian treaties.
3. Appointment of agents for Indians east of Rocky Mountains.
4. Indian agents for New Mexico.
5. For Utah

entering to upon the duties of their respective offices, shall give bond[6] in such penalties and with such security, as the President or Secretary of the Interior may require, and shall hold their offices respectively for the term four years.[7]

Sec. 7. *And be it further enacted*, That all the laws now in force, regulating trade and intercourse with the Indian tribes, or such provisions of the same as may be applicable, shall be, and the same are hereby, extended over the Indian tribes in the Territories of New Mexico Utah.[8]

Sec. 8. *And be it further enacted*, That from and after the thirtieth day of June next, the salaries of interpreters lawfully employed in the service of the United States, in California, Oregon, Utah, and New Mexico, shall be five hundred dollars per annum, and of all so employed elsewhere, four hundred dollars.

Sec. 9. *And be it further enacted*, That the chief clerk in the office of Indian affairs[9] shall be allowed a salary equal to that of thee chief clerk of any other bureau, and that the appointment of four additional met clerks[10] in said office be, and is hereby authorized, two of whom shall be allowed a salary of sixteen hundred dollars each, one a salary of fourteen hundred dollars, and one a salary of twelve hundred dollars, and that the payment of the salary of fourteen hundred dollars to one of the clerks in said office out of the Chickasaw fund be discontinued[11], and that said salary be hereafter paid out of the treasury of the United States. Nor shall further payments be made out of said fund to any clerk or clerks in any of the executive offices.

For payment of per diem of a special agent at a rate not to exceed four dollars per day, and expenses of transportation, for the purpose of paying off Indians in the old States, and particularly the North Carolina Indians, their removal and subsistence fund

---

6. Superintendents and agents to give bonds
7. To hold office for four years.
8. Former applicable laws extended to New Mexico and Utah.
9. Chief clerk in the office of Indian affairs.
10. Other clerks.
11. No clerk to be paid from the Chickasaw fund.

under the order and instructions of the Secretary of the Treasury, one thousand dollars.[12]

APPROVED, February 27, 1851.

---

12. Special agent to pay off Indians in the old states.

What to the Slave is the Fourth of July

Mr. President, Friends and Fellow Citizens:

He who could address this audience without a quailing sensation, has stronger nerves than I have. I do not remember ever to have appeared as a speaker before any assembly more shrinkingly, nor with greater distrust of my ability, than I do this day. A feeling has crept over me, quite unfavorable to the exercise of my limited powers of speech. The task before me is one which requires much previous thought and study for its proper performance. I know that apologies of this sort are generally considered flat and unmeaning. I trust, however, that mine will not be so considered. Should I seem at ease, my appearance would much misrepresent me. The little experience I have had in addressing public meetings, in country schoolhouses, avails me nothing on the present occasion.

The papers and placards say, that I am to deliver a 4th (of) July oration. This certainly sounds large, and out of the common way, for it is true that I have often had the privilege to speak in this beautiful Hall, and to address many who now honor me with their presence. But neither their familiar faces, nor the perfect gage I think I have of Corinthian Hall, seems to free me from embarrassment.

The fact is, ladies and gentlemen, the distance between this platform and the slave plantation, from which I escaped, is considerable—and the difficulties to be overcome in getting from the latter to the former, are by no means slight. That I am here today is, to me, a matter of astonishment as well as of gratitude. You will not, therefore, be surprised, if in what I have to say I evince no elaborate preparation, nor grace my speech with any high sounding exordium. With little experience and with less learning, I have been able to throw my thoughts hastily and imperfectly together; and trusting to your patient and generous indulgence, I will proceed to lay them before you.

This, for the purpose of this celebration, is the 4th of July. It is the birthday of your National Independence, and of your political freedom. This, to you, is what the Passover was to the emancipated people of God. It carries your minds back to the day, and to the act of your great deliverance; and to the signs, and to the wonders, associated with that act, and that day. This celebration also marks the beginning of another year of your national life; and reminds you that the Republic of America is now seventy-six years old. I am glad, fellow-citizens, that your nation is so young. Seventy-six years, though a good old age for a man, is but a mere speck in the life of a nation. Three score years and ten is the allotted time for individual men; but nations number their years by thousands. According to this fact, you are, even now, only in the beginning of your national career, still lingering in the period of childhood. I repeat, I am glad this is so. There is hope in the thought, and hope is much needed, under the dark clouds which lower above the horizon. The eye of the reformer is met with angry flashes, portending disastrous times; but his heart may well beat lighter at the thought that America is young, and that she is still in the impressible stage of her existence. May he not hope that high lessons of wisdom, of justice and of truth, will yet give direction to her destiny? Were the nation older, the patriot's heart might be sadder, and the reformer's brow heavier. Its future might be shrouded in gloom, and the hope of its prophets go out in sorrow. There is consolation in the thought that America is young. Great streams are not easily turned from channels, worn deep in the course of ages. They may sometimes rise in quiet and stately majesty, and inundate the land, refreshing and fertilizing the earth with their mysterious properties. They may also rise in wrath and fury, and bear away, on their angry waves, the accumulated wealth of years of toil and hardship. They, however, gradually flow back to the same old channel, and flow on as serenely as ever. But, while the river may not be turned aside, it may dry up, and leave nothing behind but the withered branch, and the unsightly rock, to howl in the abyss-sweeping wind, the sad tale of departed glory. As with rivers so with nations.

Fellow-citizens, I shall not presume to dwell at length on the associations that cluster about this day. The simple story of it is that, seventy-six years ago, the people of this country were British subjects. The style and title of your "sovereign people" (in which you now glory) was not then born. You were under the British Crown. Your fathers esteemed the English Government as the home government; and England as the fatherland. This home government, you know, although a considerable distance from your home, did, in the exercise of its parental prerogatives, impose upon its colonial children, such restraints, burdens and limitations, as, in its mature judgment, it deemed wise, right and proper.

But, your fathers, who had not adopted the fashionable idea of this day, of the infallibility of government, and the absolute character of its acts, presumed to differ from the home government in respect to the wisdom and the justice of some of those burdens and restraints. They went so far in their excitement as to pronounce the measures of government unjust, unreasonable, and oppressive, and altogether such as ought not to be quietly submitted to. I scarcely need say, fellow-citizens, that my opinion of those measures fully accords with that of your fathers. Such a declaration of agreement on my part would not be worth much to anybody. It would, certainly, prove nothing, as to what part I might have taken, had I lived during the great controversy of 1776. To say now that America was right, and England wrong, is exceedingly easy. Everybody can say it; the dastard, not less than the noble brave, can flippantly discant on the tyranny of England towards the American Colonies. It is fashionable to do so; but there was a time when to pronounce against England, and in favor of the cause of the colonies, tried men's souls. They who did so were accounted in their day, plotters of mischief, agitators and rebels, dangerous men. To side with the right, against the wrong, with the weak against the strong, and with the oppressed against the oppressor! here lies the merit, and the one which, of all others, seems unfashionable in our day. The cause of liberty may be stabbed by the men who glory in the deeds of your fathers. But, to proceed.

Feeling themselves harshly and unjustly treated by the home government, your fathers, like men of honesty, and men of spirit, earnestly sought redress. They petitioned and remonstrated; they did so in a decorous, respectful, and loyal manner. Their conduct was wholly unexceptionable. This, however, did not answer the purpose. They saw themselves treated with sovereign indifference, coldness and scorn. Yet they persevered. They were not the men to look back.

As the sheet anchor takes a firmer hold, when the ship is tossed by the storm, so did the cause of your fathers grow stronger, as it breasted the chilling blasts of kingly displeasure. The greatest and best of British statesmen admitted its justice, and the loftiest eloquence of the British Senate came to its support. But, with that blindness which seems to be the unvarying characteristic of tyrants, since Pharaoh and his hosts were drowned in the Red Sea, the British Government persisted in the exactions complained of.

The madness of this course, we believe, is admitted now, even by England; but we fear the lesson is wholly lost on our present ruler.

Oppression makes a wise man mad. Your fathers were wise men, and if they did not go mad, they became restive under this treatment. They felt themselves the victims of grievous wrongs, wholly incurable in their colonial capacity. With brave men there is always a remedy for oppression. Just here, the idea of a total separation of the colonies from the crown was born! It was a startling idea, much more so, than we, at this distance of time, regard it. The timid and the prudent (as has been intimated) of that day, were, of course, shocked and alarmed by it.

Such people lived then, had lived before, and will, probably, ever have a place on this planet; and their course, in respect to any great change, (no matter how great the good to be attained, or the wrong to be redressed by it), may be calculated with as much precision as can be the course of the stars. They hate all changes, but silver, gold and copper change! Of this sort of change they are always strongly in favor.

These people were called Tories in the days of your fathers; and the appellation, probably, conveyed the same idea that is meant by a more modern, though a somewhat less euphonious term, which we often find in our papers, applied to some of our old politicians.

Their opposition to the then dangerous thought was earnest and powerful; but, amid all their terror and affrighted vociferations against it, the alarming and revolutionary idea moved on, and the country with it.

On the 2d of July, 1776, the old Continental Congress, to the dismay of the lovers of ease, and the worshipers of property, clothed that dreadful idea with all the authority of national sanction. They did so in the form of a resolution; and as we seldom hit upon resolutions, drawn up in our day whose transparency is at all equal to this, it may refresh your minds and help my story if I read it. "Resolved, That these united colonies are, and of right, ought to be free and Independent States; that they are absolved from all allegiance to the British Crown; and that all political connection between them and the State of Great Britain is, and ought to be, dissolved."

Citizens, your fathers made good that resolution. They succeeded; and today you reap the fruits of their success. The freedom gained is yours; and you, therefore, may properly celebrate this anniversary. The 4th of July is the first great fact in your nation's history—the very ring-bolt in the chain of your yet undeveloped destiny.

Pride and patriotism, not less than gratitude, prompt you to celebrate and to hold it in perpetual remembrance. I have said that the Declaration of Independence is the ring-bolt to the chain of your nation's destiny; so, indeed, I regard it. The principles contained in that instrument are saving principles. Stand by those principles, be true to them on all occasions, in all places, against all foes, and at whatever cost.

From the round top of your ship of state, dark and threatening clouds may be seen. Heavy billows, like mountains in the distance, disclose to the leeward huge forms of flinty rocks! That bolt drawn, that chain broken, and all is lost. Cling to this day—cling to it, and to its principles, with the grasp of a storm-tossed mariner to a spar at midnight.

The coming into being of a nation, in any circumstances, is an interesting event. But, besides general considerations, there were peculiar circumstances which make the advent of this republic an event of special attractiveness.

The whole scene, as I look back to it, was simple, dignified and sublime.

The population of the country, at the time, stood at the insignificant number of three millions. The country was poor in the munitions of war. The population was weak and scattered, and the country a wilderness unsubdued. There were then no means of concert and combination, such as exist now. Neither steam nor lightning had then been reduced to order and discipline. From the Potomac to the Delaware was a journey of many days. Under these, and innumerable other disadvantages, your fathers declared for liberty and independence and triumphed.

Fellow Citizens, I am not wanting in respect for the fathers of this republic. The signers of the Declaration of Independence were brave men. They were great men too—great enough to give fame to a great age. It does not often happen to a nation to raise, at one time, such a number of truly great men. The point from which I am compelled to view them is not, certainly, the most favorable; and yet I cannot contemplate their great deeds with less than admiration. They were statesmen, patriots and heroes, and for the good they did, and the principles they contended for, I will unite with you to honor their memory.

They loved their country better than their own private interests; and, though this is not the highest form of human excellence, all will concede that it is a rare virtue, and that when it is exhibited, it ought to command respect. He who will, intelligently, lay down his life for his country, is a man whom it is not in human nature to despise. Your fathers staked their lives, their fortunes, and their sacred honor, on the cause of their country. In their admiration of liberty, they lost sight of all other interests.

They were peace men; but they preferred revolution to peaceful submission to bondage. They were quiet men; but they did not shrink from agitating against oppression. They showed forbearance; but that they knew its limits. They believed in order; but not in the order of tyranny. With them, nothing was "settled" that was not right. With them, justice, liberty and humanity were "final;" not slavery and oppression. You may well cherish the memory of such men. They were great in their day and generation. Their solid manhood stands out the more as we contrast it with these degenerate times.

How circumspect, exact and proportionate were all their movements! How unlike the politicians of an hour! Their statesmanship looked beyond the passing moment, and stretched away in strength into the distant future. They seized upon eternal principles, and set a glorious example in their defense. Mark them!

Fully appreciating the hardship to be encountered, firmly believing in the right of their cause, honorably inviting the scrutiny of an on-looking world, reverently appealing to heaven to attest their sincerity, soundly comprehending the solemn responsibility they were about to assume, wisely measuring the terrible odds against them, your fathers, the fathers of this republic, did, most deliberately, under the inspiration of a glorious patriotism, and with a sublime faith in the great principles of justice and freedom, lay deep the corner-stone of the national superstructure, which has risen and still rises in grandeur around you.

Of this fundamental work, this day is the anniversary. Our eyes are met with demonstrations of joyous enthusiasm. Banners and pennants wave exultingly on the breeze. The din of business, too, is hushed. Even Mammon seems to have quitted his grasp on this day. The ear-piercing fife and the stirring drum unite their accents with the ascending peal of a thousand church bells. Prayers are made, hymns are sung, and sermons are preached in honor of this day; while the quick martial tramp of a great and multitudinous nation, echoed back by all the hills, valleys and mountains of a vast continent, bespeak the occasion one of thrilling and universal interest—a nation's jubilee.

Friends and citizens, I need not enter further into the causes which led to this anniversary. Many of you understand them better than I do. You could instruct me in regard to them. That is a branch of knowledge in which you feel, perhaps, a much deeper interest than your speaker. The causes which led to the separation of the colonies from the British crown have never lacked for a tongue. They have all been taught in your common schools, narrated at your firesides, unfolded from your pulpits, and thundered from your legislative halls, and are as familiar to you as household words. They form the staple of your national poetry and eloquence.

I remember, also, that, as a people, Americans are remarkably familiar with all facts which make in their own favor. This is esteemed by some as a national trait—perhaps a national weakness. It is a fact, that whatever makes for the wealth or for the reputation of Americans, and can be had cheap! will be found by Americans. I shall not be charged with slandering Americans, if I say I think the American side of any question may be safely left in American hands.

I leave, therefore, the great deeds of your fathers to other gentlemen whose claim to have been regularly descended will be less likely to be disputed than mine!

My business, if I have any here today, is with the present. The accepted time with God and his cause is the ever-living now.

> *Trust no future, however pleasant,*
> *Let the dead past bury its dead;*
> *Act, act in the living present,*
> *Heart within, and God overhead.*

We have to do with the past only as we can make it useful to the present and to the future. To all inspiring motives, to noble deeds which can be gained from the past, we are welcome. But now is the time, the important time. Your fathers have lived, died, and have done their work, and have done much of it well. You live and must die, and you must do your work. You have no right to enjoy a child's share in the labor of your fathers, unless your children are to be blest by your labors. You have no right to wear out and waste the hard-earned fame of your fathers to cover your indolence. Sydney Smith tells us that men seldom eulogize the wisdom and virtues of their fathers, but to excuse some folly or wickedness of their own. This truth is not a doubtful one. There are illustrations of it near and remote, ancient and modern. It was fashionable, hundreds of years ago, for the children of Jacob to boast, we have "Abraham to our father," when they had long lost Abraham's faith and spirit. That people contented themselves under the shadow of Abraham's great name, while they repudiated the deeds which made his name great. Need I remind you that a similar thing is being done all over this country today? Need I tell you that the Jews are not the only people who built the tombs of the prophets, and garnished the sepulchres of the righteous? Washington could not die till he had broken the chains of his slaves. Yet his monument is built up by the price of human blood, and the traders in the bodies and souls of men shout—"We have Washington to *our father*."—Alas! That it should be so; yet so it is.

The evil that men do, lives after them, The good is oft-interred with their bones.

Fellow-citizens, pardon me, allow me to ask, why am I called upon to speak here today? What have I, or those I represent, to do with your national independence? Are the great principles of political freedom and of natural justice, embodied in that Declaration of Independence, extended to us? And am I, therefore, called upon to bring our humble offering to the national altar, and to confess the benefits and express devout gratitude for the blessings resulting from your independence to us?

Would to God, both for your sakes and ours, that an affirmative answer could be truthfully returned to these questions! Then would my task be light, and my burden easy and delightful. For who is there so cold, that a nation's sympathy could not warm him? Who so obdurate and dead to the claims of gratitude, that would not thankfully acknowledge such priceless benefits? Who so stolid and selfish, that would not give his voice to swell the hallelujahs of a nation's jubilee, when the chains of servitude had been torn from his limbs? I am not that man. In a case like that, the dumb might eloquently speak, and the "lame man leap as an hart."

But, such is not the state of the case. I say it with a sad sense of the disparity between us. I am not included within the pale of this glorious anniversary! Your high independence only reveals the immeasurable distance between us. The blessings in which you, this day, rejoice, are not enjoyed in common.—The rich inheritance of justice, liberty, prosperity and independence, bequeathed by your fathers, is shared by you, not by me. The sunlight that brought life and healing to you, has brought stripes and death to me. This Fourth (of) July is *yours*, not *mine*. *You* may rejoice, *I* must mourn. To drag a man in fetters into the grand illuminated temple of liberty, and call upon him to join you in joyous anthems, were inhuman mockery and sacrilegious irony. Do you mean, citizens, to mock me, by asking me to speak today? If so, there is a parallel to your conduct. And let me warn you that it is dangerous to copy the example of a nation whose crimes, lowering up to heaven, were thrown down by the breath of the Almighty, burying that nation in irrecoverable ruin! I can today take up the plaintive lament of a peeled and woe-smitten people!

"By the rivers of Babylon, there we sat down. Yea! We wept when we remembered Zion. We hanged our harps upon the willows in the midst thereof. For there, they that carried us away captive, required of us a song; and they who wasted us required of us mirth, saying, Sing us one of the songs of Zion. How can we sing the Lord's song in a strange land? If I forget thee, O Jerusalem, let my right hand forget her cunning. If I do not remember thee, let my tongue cleave to the roof of my mouth."

Fellow-citizens; above your national, tumultuous joy, I hear the mournful wail of millions! Whose chains, heavy and grievous yesterday, are, today, rendered more intolerable by the jubilee shouts that reach them. If I do forget, if I do not faithfully remember those bleeding children of sorrow this day, "may my right hand forget her cunning, and may my tongue cleave to the roof of my mouth!" To forget them, to pass lightly over their wrongs, and to chime in with the popular theme, would be treason most scandalous and shocking, and would make me a reproach before God and the world. My subject, then, fellow-citizens, is AMERICAN SLAVERY. I shall see, this day, and its popular characteristics, from the slave's point of view. Standing, there, identified with the American bondman, making his wrongs mine, I do not hesitate to declare, with all my soul, that the character and conduct of this nation never looked blacker to me than on this 4th of July! Whether we turn to the declarations of the past, or to the professions of the present, the conduct of the nation seems equally hideous and revolting. America is false to the past, false to the present, and solemnly binds herself to be false to the future. Standing with God and the crushed and bleeding slave on this occasion, I will, in the name of humanity which is outraged, in the name of liberty which is fettered, in the name of the constitution and the Bible, which are disregarded and trampled upon, dare to call in question and to denounce, with all the emphasis I can command, everything that serves to perpetuate slavery—the great sin and shame of America! "I will not equivocate; I will not excuse;" I will use the severest language I can command; and yet not one word shall escape me that any man, whose judgment is not blinded by prejudice, or who is not at heart a slaveholder, shall not confess to be right and just.

But I fancy I hear some one of my audience say, it is just in this circumstance that you and your brother abolitionists fail to make a favorable impression on the public mind. Would you argue more, and denounce less, would you persuade more, and rebuke less, your cause would be much more likely to succeed. But, I submit, where all is plain there is nothing to be argued. What point in the anti-slavery creed would you have me argue? On what branch of the subject do the people of this country need light? Must I undertake to prove that the slave is a man? That point is conceded already. Nobody doubts it. The slaveholders themselves acknowledge it in the enactment of laws for their government. They acknowledge it when they punish disobedience on the part of the slave. There are seventy-two crimes in the State of Virginia, which, if committed by a black man, (no matter how ignorant he be), subject him to the punishment of death; while only two of the same crimes will subject a white man to the like punishment. What is this but the acknowledgement that the slave is a moral, intellectual and responsible being? The manhood of the slave is conceded. It is admitted in the fact that Southern statute books are covered with enactments forbidding, under severe fines and penalties, the teaching of the slave to read or to write. When you can point to any such laws, in reference to the beasts of the field, then I may consent to argue the manhood of the slave. When the dogs in your streets, when the fowls of the air, when the cattle on your hills, when the fish of the sea, and the reptiles that crawl, shall be unable to distinguish the slave from a brute, *then* will I argue with you that the slave is a man!

For the present, it is enough to affirm the equal manhood of the Negro race. Is it not astonishing that, while we are ploughing, planting and reaping, using all kinds of mechanical tools, erecting houses, constructing bridges, building ships, working in metals of brass, iron, copper, silver and gold; that, while we are reading, writing and cyphering, acting as clerks, merchants and secretaries, having among us lawyers, doctors, ministers, poets, authors, editors, orators and teachers; that, while we are engaged in all manner of enterprises common to other men, digging gold in California, capturing the whale in the Pacific, feeding sheep and cattle on the hill-side, living, moving, acting, thinking, planning, living in families as husbands, wives and children, and, above all, confessing and worshipping the Christian's God, and looking hopefully for life and immortality beyond the grave, we are called upon to prove that we are men!

Would you have me argue that man is entitled to liberty? that he is the rightful owner of his own body? You have already declared it. Must I argue the wrongfulness of slavery? Is that a question for Republicans? Is it to be settled by the rules of logic and argumentation, as a matter beset with great difficulty, involving a doubtful application of the principle of justice, hard to be understood? How should I look today, in the presence of Americans, dividing, and subdividing a discourse, to show that men have a natural right to freedom? Speaking of it relatively, and positively, negatively, and affirmatively. To do so, would be to make myself ridiculous, and to offer an insult to your understanding.— There is not a man beneath the canopy of heaven, that does not know that slavery is wrong *for him*.

What, am I to argue that it is wrong to make men brutes, to rob them of their liberty, to work them without wages, to keep them ignorant of their relations to their fellow men, to beat them with sticks, to flay their flesh with the lash, to load their limbs with irons, to hunt them with dogs, to sell them at auction, to sunder their families, to knock out their teeth, to burn their flesh, to starve them into obedience and submission to their masters? Must I argue that a system thus marked with blood, and stained with pollution, is *wrong*? No! I will not. I have better employments for my time and strength than such arguments would imply.

What, then, remains to be argued? Is it that slavery is not divine; that God did not establish it; that our doctors of divinity are mistaken? There is blasphemy in the thought. That which is inhuman, cannot be divine! Who can reason on such a proposition? They that can, may; I cannot. The time for such argument is passed.

At a time like this, scorching irony, not convincing argument, is needed. O! had I the ability, and could I reach the nation's ear, I would, today, pour out a fiery stream of biting ridicule, blasting reproach, withering sarcasm, and stern rebuke. For it is not light that is needed, but fire; it is not the gentle shower, but thunder. We need the storm, the whirlwind, and the earthquake. The feeling of the nation must be quickened; the conscience of the nation must be roused; the propriety of the nation must be startled; the hypocrisy of the nation must be exposed; and its crimes against God and man must be proclaimed and denounced.

What, to the American slave, is your 4th of July? I answer: a day that reveals to him, more than all other days in the year, the gross injustice and cruelty to which he is the constant victim. To him, your celebration is a sham; your boasted liberty, an unholy license; your national greatness, swelling vanity; your sounds of rejoicing are empty and heartless; your denunciations of tyrants, brass fronted impudence; your shouts of liberty and equality, hollow mockery; your prayers and hymns, your sermons and thanksgivings, with all your religious parade, and solemnity, are, to him, mere bombast, fraud, deception, impiety, and hypocrisy—a thin veil to cover up crimes which would disgrace a nation of savages. There is not a nation on the earth guilty of practices, more shocking and bloody, than are the people of these United States, at this very hour.

Go where you may, search where you will, roam through all the monarchies and despotisms of the old world, travel through

South America, search out every abuse, and when you have found the last, lay your facts by the side of the everyday practices of this nation, and you will say with me, that, for revolting barbarity and shameless hypocrisy, America reigns without a rival.

Take the American slave-trade, which, we are told by the papers, is especially prosperous just now. Ex-Senator Benton tells us that the price of men was never higher than now. He mentions the fact to show that slavery is in no danger. This trade is one of the peculiarities of American institutions. It is carried on in all the large towns and cities in one-half of this confederacy; and millions are pocketed every year, by dealers in this horrid traffic. In several states, this trade is a chief source of wealth. It is called (in contradistinction to the foreign slave-trade) "*the internal slave trade*." It is, probably, called so, too, in order to divert from it the horror with which the foreign slave-trade is contemplated. That trade has long since been denounced by this government, as piracy. It has been denounced with burning words, from the high places of the nation, as an execrable traffic. To arrest it, to put an end to it, this nation keeps a squadron, at immense cost, on the coast of Africa. Everywhere, in this country, it is safe to speak of this foreign slave-trade, as a most inhuman traffic, opposed alike to the laws of God and of man. The duty to extirpate and destroy it, is admitted even by our DOCTORS OF DIVINITY. In order to put an end to it, some of these last have consented that their colored brethren (nominally free) should leave this country, and establish themselves on the western coast of Africa! It is, however, a notable fact that, while so much execration is poured out by Americans upon those engaged in the foreign slave-trade, the men engaged in the slave-trade between the states pass without condemnation, and their business is deemed honorable.

Behold the practical operation of this internal slave-trade, the American slave-trade, sustained by American politics and America religion. Here you will see men and women reared like swine for the market. You know what is a swine-drover? I will show you a man-drover. They inhabit all our Southern States. They perambulate the country, and crowd the highways of the nation, with droves of human stock. You will see one of these human flesh-jobbers, armed with pistol, whip and bowie-knife, driving a company of a hundred men, women, and children, from the Potomac to the slave market at New Orleans. These wretched people are to be sold singly, or in lots, to suit purchasers. They are food for the cotton-field, and the deadly sugar-mill. Mark the sad procession, as it moves wearily along, and the inhuman wretch who drives them. Hear his savage yells and his blood-chilling oaths, as he hurries on his affrighted captives! There, see the old man, with locks thinned and gray. Cast one glance, if you please, upon that young mother, whose shoulders are bare to the scorching sun, her briny tears falling on the brow of the babe in her arms. See, too, that girl of thirteen, weeping, *yes*! Weeping, as she thinks of the mother from whom she has been torn! The drove moves tardily. Heat and sorrow have nearly consumed their strength; suddenly you hear a quick snap, like the discharge of a rifle; the fetters clank, and the chain rattles simultaneously; your ears are saluted with a scream, that seems to have torn its way to the center of your soul! The crack you heard, was the sound of the slave-whip; the scream you heard, was from the woman you saw with the babe. Her speed had faltered under the weight of her child and her chains! That gash on her shoulder tells her to move on. Follow the drove to New Orleans. Attend the auction; see men examined like horses; see the forms of women rudely and brutally exposed to the shocking gaze of American slave-buyers. See this drove sold and separated forever; and never forget the deep, sad sobs that arose from that scattered multitude. Tell me citizens, WHERE, under the sun, you can witness a spectacle more fiendish and shocking. Yet this is but a glance at the American slave-trade, as it exists, at this moment, in the ruling part of the United States.

I was born amid such sights and scenes. To me the American slave-trade is a terrible reality. When a child, my soul was often pierced with a sense of its horrors. I lived on Philpot Street, Fell's Point, Baltimore, and have watched from the wharves, the slave ships in the Basin, anchored from the shore, with their cargoes of human flesh, waiting for favorable winds to waft them down the Chesapeake. There was, at that time, a grand slave mart kept at the head of Pratt Street, by Austin Woldfolk. His agents were sent into every town and county in Maryland, announcing their arrival, through the papers, and on flaming "*hand-bills*," headed CASH FOR NEGROES. These men were generally well dressed men, and very captivating in their manners. Ever ready to drink, to treat, and to gamble. The fate of many a slave has depended upon the turn of a single card; and many a child has been snatched from the arms of its mother by bargains arranged in a state of brutal drunkenness.

The flesh-mongers gather up their victims by dozens, and drive them, chained, to the general depot at Baltimore. When a sufficient number have been collected here, a ship is chartered, for the purpose of conveying the forlorn crew to Mobile, or to New Orleans. From the slave prison to the ship, they are usually driven in the darkness of night; for since the antislavery agitation, a certain caution is observed.

In the deep still darkness of midnight, I have been often aroused by the dead heavy footsteps, and the piteous cries of the chained gangs that passed our door. The anguish of my boyish heart was intense; and I was often consoled, when speaking to my mistress in the morning, to hear her say that the custom was very wicked; that she hated to hear the rattle of the chains, and the heart-rending cries. I was glad to find one who sympathized with me in my horror.

Fellow-citizens, this murderous traffic is, today, in active operation in this boasted republic. In the solitude of my spirit, I see clouds of dust raised on the highways of the South; I see the bleeding footsteps; I hear the doleful wail of fettered humanity, on the way to the slave-markets, where the victims are to be sold like *horses*, *sheep*, and *swine*, knocked off to the highest bidder. There I see the tenderest ties ruthlessly broken, to gratify the lust, caprice and rapacity of the buyers and sellers of men. My soul sickens at the sight.

> *Is this the land your Fathers loved,*
> *The freedom which they toiled to win?*
> *Is this the earth whereon they moved?*
> *Are these the graves they slumber in?*

But a still more inhuman, disgraceful, and scandalous state of things remains to be presented. By an act of the American Congress, not yet two years old, slavery has been nationalized in its most horrible and revolting form. By that act, Mason and Dixon's line has been obliterated; New York has become as Virginia; and the power to hold, hunt, and sell men, women, and children as slaves remains no longer a mere state institution, but is now an institution of the whole United States. The power is co-extensive with the Star-Spangled Banner and American Christianity. Where these go, may also go the merciless slave-hunter. Where these are, man is not sacred. He is a bird for the sportsman's gun. By that most foul and fiendish of all human decrees, the liberty and person of every man are put in peril. Your broad republican domain is hunting ground for *men*. Not for thieves and robbers, enemies of society, merely, but for men guilty of no crime. Your lawmakers have commanded all good citizens to engage in this hellish sport. Your President, your Secretary of State, our *lords*, *nobles*, and ecclesiastics, enforce, as a duty you owe to your free and glorious country, and to your God, that you do this accursed thing. Not fewer than forty Americans have, within the past two years, been hunted down and, without a moment's warning, hurried away in chains, and consigned to slavery and excruciating torture. Some of these have had wives and children, dependent on them for bread; but of this, no account was made. The right of the hunter to his prey stands superior to the right of marriage, and to *all* rights in this republic, the rights of God included! For black men there are neither law, justice, humanity, not religion. The Fugitive Slave *Law* makes mercy to them a crime; and bribes the judge who tries them. An American judge gets ten dollars for every victim he consigns to slavery, and five, when he fails to do so. The oath of any two villains is sufficient, under this hell-black enactment, to send the most pious and exemplary black man into the remorseless jaws of slavery! His own testimony is nothing. He can bring no witnesses for himself. The minister of American justice is bound by the law to hear but *one* side; and *that* side, is the side of the oppressor. Let this damning fact be perpetually told. Let it be thundered around the world, that, in tyrant-killing, king-hating, people-loving, democratic, Christian America, the seats of justice are filled with judges, who hold their offices under an open and palpable *bribe*, and are bound, in deciding in the case of a man's liberty, *hear only his accusers*!

In glaring violation of justice, in shameless disregard of the forms of administering law, in cunning arrangement to entrap the defenseless, and in diabolical intent, this Fugitive Slave Law stands alone in the annals of tyrannical legislation. I doubt if there be another nation on the globe, having the brass and the baseness to put such a law on the statute-book. If any man in this assembly thinks differently from me in this matter, and feels able to disprove my statements, I will gladly confront him at any suitable time and place he may select.

I take this law to be one of the grossest infringements of Christian Liberty, and, if the churches and ministers of our country were not stupidly blind, or most wickedly indifferent, they, too, would so regard it.

At the very moment that they are thanking God for the enjoyment of civil and religious liberty, and for the right to worship God according to the dictates of their own consciences, they are utterly silent in respect to a law which robs religion of its chief significance, and makes it utterly worthless to a world lying in wickedness. Did this law concern the "*mint, anise, and cumin*"—abridge the right to sing psalms, to partake of the sacrament, or to engage in any of the ceremonies of religion, it would be smitten by the thunder of a thousand pulpits. A general shout would go up from the church, demanding *repeal, repeal, instant repeal*!—And it would go hard with that politician who presumed to solicit the votes of the people without inscribing this motto on his banner. Further, if this demand were not complied with, another Scotland would be added to the history of religious liberty, and the stern old Covenanters would be thrown into the shade. A John Knox would be seen at every church door, and heard from every pulpit, and Fillmore would have no more quarter than was shown by Knox, to the beautiful, but treacherous queen Mary of Scotland. The fact that the church of our country, (with fractional exceptions), does not esteem "the Fugitive Slave

Law" as a declaration of war against religious liberty, implies that that church regards religion simply as a form of worship, an empty ceremony, and *not* a vital principle, requiring active benevolence, justice, love and good will towards man. It esteems sacrifice above mercy; psalm-singing above right doing; solemn meetings above practical righteousness. A worship that can be conducted by persons who refuse to give shelter to the houseless, to give bread to the hungry, clothing to the naked, and who enjoin obedience to a law forbidding these acts of mercy, is a curse, not a blessing to mankind. The Bible addresses all such persons as "scribes, Pharisees, hypocrites, who pay tithe of *mint*, *anise*, and *cumin*, and have omitted the weightier matters of the law, judgment, mercy and faith."

But the church of this country is not only indifferent to the wrongs of the slave, it actually takes sides with the oppressors. It has made itself the bulwark of American slavery, and the shield of American slave-hunters. Many of its most eloquent Divines. who stand as the very lights of the church, have shamelessly given the sanction of religion and the Bible to the whole slave system. They have taught that man may, properly, be a slave; that the relation of master and slave is ordained of God; that to send back an escaped bondman to his master is clearly the duty of all the followers of the Lord Jesus Christ; and this horrible blasphemy is palmed off upon the world for Christianity.

For my part, I would say, welcome infidelity! Welcome atheism! welcome anything! In preference to the gospel, *as preached by those Divines*! They convert the very name of religion into an engine of tyranny, and barbarous cruelty, and serve to confirm more infidels, in this age, than all the infidel writings of Thomas Paine, Voltaire, and Bolingbroke, put together, have done! These ministers make religion a cold and flinty-hearted thing, having neither principles of right action, nor bowels of compassion. They strip the love of God of its beauty, and leave the throng of religion a huge, horrible, repulsive form. It is a religion for oppressors, tyrants, man-stealers, and *thugs*. It is not that "*pure and undefiled religion*" which is from above, and which is "*first pure, then peaceable, easy to be entreated*, full of mercy and good fruits, *without partiality, and without hypocrisy*." But a religion which favors the rich against the poor; which exalts the proud above the humble; which divides mankind into two classes, tyrants and slaves; which says to the man in chains, *stay there*; and to the oppressor, *oppress on*; it is a religion which may be professed and enjoyed by all the robbers and enslavers of mankind; it makes God a respecter of persons, denies his fatherhood of the race, and tramples in the dust the great truth of the brotherhood of man. All this we affirm to be true of the popular church, and the popular worship of our land and nation—a religion, a church, and a worship which, on the authority of inspired wisdom, we pronounce to be an abomination in the sight of God. In the language of Isaiah, the American church might be well addressed, "Bring no more vain ablations; incense is an abomination unto me: the new moons and Sabbaths, the calling of assemblies, I cannot away with; it is iniquity even the solemn meeting. Your new moons and your appointed feasts my soul hateth. They are a trouble to me; I am weary to bear them; and when ye spread forth your hands I will hide mine eyes from you. Yea! When ye make many prayers, I will not hear. YOUR HANDS ARE FULL OF BLOOD; cease to do evil, learn to do well; seek judgment; relieve the oppressed; judge for the fatherless; plead for the widow."

The American church is guilty, when viewed in connection with what it is doing to uphold slavery; but it is superlatively guilty when viewed in connection with its ability to abolish slavery. The sin of which it is guilty is one of omission as well as of commission. Albert Barnes but uttered what the common sense of every man at all observant of the actual state of the case will receive as truth, when he declared that "There is no power out of the church that could sustain slavery an hour, if it were not sustained in it."

Let the religious press, the pulpit, the Sunday school, the conference meeting, the great ecclesiastical, missionary, Bible and tract associations of the land array their immense powers against slavery and slave-holding; and the whole system of crime and blood would be scattered to the winds; and that they do not do this involves them in the most awful responsibility of which the mind can conceive.

In prosecuting the anti-slavery enterprise, we have been asked to spare the church, to spare the ministry; but *how*, we ask, could such a thing be done? We are met on the threshold of our efforts for the redemption of the slave, by the church and ministry of the country, in battle arrayed against us; and we are compelled to fight or flee. From *what* quarter, I beg to know, has proceeded a fire so deadly upon our ranks, during the last two years, as from the Northern pulpit? As the champions of oppressors, the chosen men of American theology have appeared—men, honored for their so-called piety, and their real learning. The Lords of Buffalo, the Springs of New York, the Lathrops of Auburn, the Coxes and Spencers of Brooklyn, the Gannets and Sharps of Boston, the Deweys of Washington, and other great religious lights of the land have, in utter denial of the authority of *Him* by whom they professed to be called to the ministry, deliberately taught us, against the example or the Hebrews and against the remonstrance of the Apostles, they teach *that we ought to obey man's law before the law of God*.

My spirit wearies of such blasphemy; and how such men can be supported, as the "standing types and representatives of Jesus Christ," is a mystery which I leave others to penetrate. In speaking of the American church, however, let it be distinctly understood that I mean the great mass of the religious organizations of our land. There are exceptions, and I thank God that there are. Noble men may be found, scattered all over these Northern States, of whom Henry Ward Beecher of Brooklyn, Samuel J. May of Syracuse, and my esteemed friend (Rev. R. R. Raymond) on the platform, are shining examples; and let me say further, that upon these men lies the duty to inspire our ranks with high religious faith and zeal, and to cheer us on in the great mission of the slave's redemption from his chains.

One is struck with the difference between the attitude of the American church towards the anti-slavery movement, and that occupied by the churches in England towards a similar movement in that country. There, the church, true to its mission of ameliorating, elevating, and improving the condition of mankind, came forward promptly, bound up the wounds of the

West Indian slave, and restored him to his liberty. There, the question of emancipation was a high religious question. It was demanded, in the name of humanity, and according to the law of the living God. The Sharps, the Clarksons, the Wilberforces, the Buxtons, and Burchells and the Knibbs, were alike famous for their piety, and for their philanthropy. The anti-slavery movement *there* was not an anti-church movement, for the reason that the church took its full share in prosecuting that movement: and the anti-slavery movement in this country will cease to be an anti-church movement, when the church of this country shall assume a favorable, instead of a hostile position towards that movement. Americans! your republican politics, not less than your republican religion, are flagrantly inconsistent. You boast of your love of liberty, your superior civilization, and your pure Christianity, while the whole political power of the nation (as embodied in the two great political parties), is solemnly pledged to support and perpetuate the enslavement of three millions of your countrymen. You hurl your anathemas at the crowned headed tyrants of Russia and Austria, and pride yourselves on your Democratic institutions, while you yourselves consent to be the mere *tools* and *body-guards* of the tyrants of Virginia and Carolina. You invite to your shores fugitives of oppression from abroad, honor them with banquets, greet them with ovations, cheer them, toast them, salute them, protect them, and pour out your money to them like water; but the fugitives from your own land you advertise, hunt, arrest, shoot and kill. You glory in your refinement and your universal education yet you maintain a system as barbarous and dreadful as ever stained the character of a nation—a system begun in avarice, supported in pride, and perpetuated in cruelty. You shed tears over fallen Hungary, and make the sad story of her wrongs the theme of your poets, statesmen and orators, till your gallant sons are ready to fly to arms to vindicate her cause against her oppressors; but, in regard to the ten thousand wrongs of the American slave, you would enforce the strictest silence, and would hail him as an enemy of the nation who dares to make those wrongs the subject of public discourse! You are all on fire at the mention of liberty for France or for Ireland; but are as cold as an iceberg at the thought of liberty for the enslaved of America. You discourse eloquently on the dignity of labor; yet, you sustain a system which, in its very essence, casts a stigma upon labor. You can bare your bosom to the storm of British artillery to throw off a threepenny tax on tea; and yet wring the last hard-earned farthing from the grasp of the black laborers of your country. You profess to believe "that, of one blood, God made all nations of men to dwell on the face of all the earth," and hath commanded all men, everywhere to love one another; yet you notoriously hate, (and glory in your hatred), all men whose skins are not colored like your own. You declare, before the world, and are understood by the world to declare, that you "*hold these truths to be self evident, that all men are created equal; and are endowed by their Creator with certain inalienable rights; and that, among these are, life, liberty, and the pursuit of happiness*;" and yet, you hold securely, in a bondage which, according to your own Thomas Jefferson, "*is worse than ages of that which your fathers rose in rebellion to oppose*," a *seventh part* of the inhabitants of your country.

Fellow-citizens! I will not enlarge further on your national inconsistencies. The existence of slavery in this country brands your republicanism as a sham, your humanity as a base pretence, and your Christianity as a lie. It destroys your moral power abroad; it corrupts your politicians at home. It saps the foundation of religion; it makes your name a hissing, and a bye-word to a mocking earth. It is the antagonistic force in your government, the only thing that seriously disturbs and endangers your *Union*. It fetters your progress; it is the enemy of improvement, the deadly foe of education; it fosters pride; it breeds insolence; it promotes vice; it shelters crime; it is a curse to the earth that supports it; and yet, you cling to it, as if it were the sheet anchor of all your hopes. Oh! Be warned! Be warned! A horrible reptile is coiled up in your nation's bosom; the venomous creature is nursing at the tender breast of your youthful republic; *for the love of God*, tear away, and fling from you the hideous monster, and *let the weight of twenty millions crush and destroy it forever*!

But it is answered in reply to all this, that precisely what I have now denounced is, in fact, guaranteed and sanctioned by the

Constitution of the United States; that the right to hold and to hunt slaves is a part of that Constitution framed by the illustrious Fathers of this Republic.

Then, I dare to affirm, notwithstanding all I have said before, your fathers stooped, basely stooped

> *To palter with us in a double sense:*
> *And keep the word of promise to the ear,*
> *But break it to the heart.*

And instead of being the honest men I have before declared them to be, they were the veriest imposters that ever practiced on mankind. This is the inevitable conclusion, and from it there is no escape. But I differ from those who charge this baseness on the framers of the Constitution of the United States. It is a slander upon their memory, at least, so I believe. There is not time now to argue the constitutional question at length—nor have I the ability to discuss it as it ought to be discussed. The subject has been handled with masterly power by Lysander Spooner, Esq., by William Goodell, by Samuel E. Sewall, Esq., and last, though not least, by Gerritt Smith, Esq. These gentlemen have, as I think, fully and clearly vindicated the Constitution from any design to support slavery for an hour.

Fellow-citizens! There is no matter in respect to which, the people of the North have allowed themselves to be so ruinously imposed upon, as that of the pro-slavery character of the Constitution. In that instrument I hold there is neither warrant, license, nor sanction of the hateful thing; but, interpreted as it ought to be interpreted, the Constitution is a GLORIOUS LIBERTY DOCUMENT. Read its preamble, consider its purposes. Is slavery among them? Is it at the gateway? Or is it in the temple? It is neither. While I do not intend to argue this question on the present occasion, let me ask, if it be not somewhat singular that, if the Constitution were intended to be, by its framers and adopters, a slave-holding instrument, why neither slavery, slaveholding, nor slave can anywhere be found in it. What would be thought of an instrument, drawn up, legally drawn up, for the purpose of entitling the city of Rochester to a track of land, in which no mention of land was made? Now, there are certain rules of interpretation, for the proper understanding of all legal instruments. These rules are well established. They are plain, common-sense rules, such as you and I, and all of us, can understand and apply, without having passed years in the study of law. I scout the idea that the question of the constitutionality or unconstitutionality of slavery is not a question for the people. I hold that every American citizen has a right to form an opinion of the constitution, and to propagate that opinion, and to use all honorable means to make his opinion the prevailing one. Without this right, the liberty of an American citizen would be as insecure as that of a Frenchman. Ex-Vice-President Dallas tells us that the Constitution is an object to which no American mind can be too attentive, and no American heart too devoted. He further says, the Constitution, in its words, is plain and intelligible, and is meant for the home-bred, unsophisticated understandings of our fellow-citizens. Senator Berrien tell us that the Constitution is the fundamental law, that which controls all others. The charter of our liberties, which every citizen has a personal interest in understanding thoroughly. The testimony of Senator Breese, Lewis Cass, and many others that might be named, who are everywhere esteemed as sound lawyers, so regard the constitution. I take it, therefore, that it is not presumption in a private citizen to form an opinion of that instrument.

Now, take the Constitution according to its plain reading, and I defy the presentation of a single pro-slavery clause in it. On the other hand it will be found to contain principles and purposes, entirely hostile to the existence of slavery.

I have detained my audience entirely too long already. At some future period I will gladly avail myself of an opportunity to give this subject a full and fair discussion.

Allow me to say, in conclusion, notwithstanding the dark picture I have this day presented of the state of the nation, I do not despair of this country. There are forces in operation, which must inevitably work the downfall of slavery. "The arm of the Lord is not shortened," and the doom of slavery is certain. I, therefore, leave off where I began, with hope. While drawing encouragement from the Declaration of Independence, the great principles it contains, and the genius of American Institutions, my spirit is also cheered by the obvious tendencies of the age. Nations do not now stand in the same relation to each other that they did ages ago. No nation can now shut itself up from the surrounding world, and trot round in the same old path of its fathers without interference. The time was when such could be done. Long established customs of hurtful character could formerly fence themselves in, and do their evil work with social impunity. Knowledge was then confined and enjoyed by the privileged few, and the multitude walked on in mental darkness. But a change has now come over the affairs of mankind. Walled cities and empires have become unfashionable. The arm of commerce has borne away the gates of the strong city. Intelligence is penetrating the darkest corners of the globe. It makes its pathway over and under the sea, as well as on the earth. Wind, steam, and lightning are its chartered agents. Oceans no longer divide, but link nations together. From Boston to London is now a holiday excursion. Space is comparatively annihilated. Thoughts expressed on one side of the Atlantic, are distinctly heard on the other. The far off and almost fabulous Pacific rolls in grandeur at our feet. The Celestial Empire, the mystery of ages, is being solved. The fiat of the Almighty, "Let there be Light," has not yet spent its force. No abuse, no outrage whether in taste, sport or avarice, can now hide itself from the all-pervading light. The iron shoe, and crippled foot of China must be seen, in contrast with nature. Africa must rise and put on her yet unwoven garment. "Ethiopia shall stretch out her hand unto God." In the fervent aspirations of William Lloyd Garrison, I say, and let every heart join in saying it:

> *God speed the year of jubilee*
> *The wide world o'er*
> *When from their galling chains set free,*
> *Th' oppress'd shall vilely bend the knee,*
> *And wear the yoke of tyranny*

Like brutes no more.
That year will come, and freedom's reign,
To man his plundered fights again
Restore.

God speed the day when human blood
Shall cease to flow!
In every clime be understood,
The claims of human brotherhood,
And each return for evil, good,
Not blow for blow;
That day will come all feuds to end.
And change into a faithful friend
Each foe.

God speed the hour, the glorious hour,
When none on earth
Shall exercise a lordly power,
Nor in a tyrant's presence cower;
But all to manhood's stature tower,
By equal birth!
That hour will come, to each, to all,
And from his prison-house, the thrall.

Go forth.
Until that year, day, hour, arrive,
With head, and heart, and hand I'll strive,
To break the rod, and rend the gyve,
The spoiler of his prey deprive—
So witness Heaven!
And never from my chosen post,
Whate'er the peril or the cost,
Be driven.

The Emancipation Proclamation

January 1, 1863

A Proclamation

WHEREAS, ON THE TWENTY-SECOND DAY of September, in the year of our Lord one thousand eight hundred and sixty-two, a proclamation was issued by the President of the United States, containing, among other things, the following, to wit:

"That on the first day of January, in the year of our Lord one thousand eight hundred and sixty-three, all persons held as slaves within any State or designated part of a State, the people whereof shall then be in rebellion against the United States, shall be then, thenceforward, and forever free; and the Executive Government of the United States, including the military and naval authority thereof, will recognize and maintain the freedom of such persons, and will do no act or acts to repress such persons, or any of them, in any efforts they may make for their actual freedom.

"That the Executive will, on the first day of January aforesaid, by proclamation, designate the States and parts of States, if any, in which the people thereof, respectively, shall then be in rebellion against the United States; and the fact that any State, or the people thereof, shall on that day be, in good faith, represented in the Congress of the United States by members chosen thereto at elections wherein a majority of the qualified voters of such State shall have participated, shall, in the absence of strong countervailing testimony, be deemed conclusive evidence that such State, and the people thereof, are not then in rebellion against the United States."

Now, therefore I, Abraham Lincoln, President of the United States, by virtue of the power in me vested as Commander-in-Chief, of the Army and Navy of the United States in time of actual armed rebellion against the authority and government of the United States, and as a fit and necessary war measure for suppressing said rebellion, do, on this first day of January, in the year of our Lord one thousand eight hundred and sixty-three, and in accordance with my purpose so to do publicly proclaimed for the full period of one hundred days, from the day first above mentioned, order and designate as the States and parts of States wherein the people thereof respectively, are this day in rebellion against the United States, the following, to wit:

Arkansas, Texas, Louisiana, (except the Parishes of St. Bernard, Plaquemines, Jefferson, St. John, St. Charles, St. James Ascension, Assumption, Terrebonne, Lafourche, St. Mary, St. Martin, and Orleans, including the City of New Orleans) Mississippi, Alabama, Florida, Georgia, South Carolina, North Carolina, and Virginia, (except the forty-eight counties designated as West Virginia, and also the counties of Berkley, Accomac, Northampton, Elizabeth City, York, Princess Ann, and Norfolk, including the cities of Norfolk and Portsmouth()), and which excepted parts, are for the present, left precisely as if this proclamation were not issued.

And by virtue of the power, and for the purpose aforesaid, I do order and declare that all persons held as slaves within said designated States, and parts of States, are, and henceforward shall be free; and that the Executive government of the United States, including the military and naval authorities thereof, will recognize and maintain the freedom of said persons.

And I hereby enjoin upon the people so declared to be free to abstain from all violence, unless in necessary self-defence; and I recommend to them that, in all cases when allowed, they labor faithfully for reasonable wages.

And I further declare and make known, that such persons of suitable condition, will be received into the armed service of the United States to garrison forts, positions, stations, and other places, and to man vessels of all sorts in said service.

And upon this act, sincerely believed to be an act of justice, warranted by the Constitution, upon military necessity, I invoke the considerate judgment of mankind, and the gracious favor of Almighty God.

In witness whereof, I have hereunto set my hand and caused the seal of the United States to be affixed.

Done at the City of Washington, this first day of January, in the year of our Lord one thousand eight hundred and sixty three, and of the Independence of the United States of America the eighty-seventh.

> By the President: ABRAHAM LINCOLN
> WILLIAM H. SEWARD, Secretary of State.
> APPROVED, May 28, 1830.

General Order No. 3

The people are informed that in accordance with a Proclamation from the Executive of the United States, all slaves are free. This involves an absolute equality of personal rights and rights of property, between former masters and slaves, and the connection heretofore existing between them, become that between employer and hired labor. The freed are advised to remain at their present homes, and work for wages. They are informed that they will not be allowed to collect at military posts; and that they will not be supported in idleness either there or elsewhere.

The Indian Appropriations Act
(Continued)

1871

An act making Appropriations for the current and contingent Expenses of the Indian Department, and for fulfilling Treaty Stipulations with various Indian Tribes, for the Year ending June thirty, eighteen hundred and seventy-two, and for other Purposes.

Be it enacted by the Senate and House of Representatives of the United States of America in Congress assembled, That the following sums be, and they are hereby, appropriated, out of any money in the treasury not otherwise appropriated, for the purpose of paying the current and contingent expenses of the Indian department, and fulfilling treaty stipulations with the various Indian tribes:—

For pay of eight superintendents of Indian affairs, namely: Two super-intendents for the tribes east of the Rocky mountains; one for Oregon; one for Washington Territory; one for the Territory of New Mexico; one for California; one for the Territory of Arizona; and one for Montana, nineteen thousand one hundred dollars.

For pay of sixty-two agents of Indian affairs, namely: Three for the tribes in Oregon; four for the tribes In New Mexico; one additional for Indiana in New Mexico; one for the tribes in New Mexico; one for the tribes in Utah; one additional for the Indiana in Utah; one for the tribes in the Territory of Utah; eleven for the tribes east of the Rocky mountains; two for the tribes east of the Rocky mountains; six for the Indiana east of the Rocky mountains; namely, Sioux, Seminole, Omaha, Kickapoo, Kansas, and Neosho agencies; three for the tribes east of the Rocky mountains; one for the Indians in the State of New York; one for Green bay, Wisconsin; three for the tribes in Washington Territory; one for the Wichitas and neighboring tribes west of the Choctaws and Chickasaws; one for the tribes east of the Rocky mountains; one for the Indians in the Territory of New Mexico; one for the Ponca tribe; one for the Pawnees; one for the Yankton Sioux;

three for the tribes in the Territory of Washington; one for the Grand River and Uintah bands of Indiana in the Territory of Colorado; two for the Upper Missouri and the country adjacent thereto; one for the Ottawas, Chippewas of Swan creek and Black river, and Christian Indians in Kansas; three agents for the State of California; one for the Kiowa, Apache, and Indian Comanche Indians; one for the Sisseton and Wahpeton bands of Dakota or Sioux Indians; one for the bands of Sacs and Foxes of the Mississippi, now in Tama county, Iowa; one for the Indians in the State of Nevada; one for the Crow tribe of Indians; one for the Shoshones and Bannocks; and one for the Sioux Indians of Devil's lake, ninety-three thousand six hundred dollars: *Provided* That it shall be the duty of the President to dispense with the services of such Indian agents and superintendents herein mentioned as may be practicable; and where it is practicable, he shall require the same person to perform the duties of two with agencies or superintendencies for one salary.

For pay of six special agents: One for the Pueblo Indians in New Mexico; one for the Moquis Pueblos in Arizona; one for the Pi-Utes in Nevada; one for the Papagoes and others in Arizona; one for the Colorado River agency; and one for the Bannocks and others at the Fort Hall reservation in Idaho Territory, nine thousand dollars.

For six sub-agents: Four for the tribes in Oregon, and two for the tribes in Washington Territory, six thousand dollars.

For pay dollars to superintendent for California, one thousand eight hundred dollars.

For temporary clerks to superintendent, six thousand six hundred dollars.

For pay of ninety interpreters, as follows: Twenty-one for the tribes in Oregon and the Territories of Washington, Utah, and New Mexico, at five hundred dollars each; thirty-six for the tribes elsewhere, at four hundred dollars each; seventeen extra for the tribes elsewhere, at four hundred dollars each; three for the Indian service in Utah, at five hundred dollars each; one for the Shoshones and one for the Utahs, at one thousand dollars each; one for the Sisseton and Wahpeton bands of Sioux, four hundred dollars; and one for the Sacs and Foxes of the Mississippi, now in Tama county, Iowa, four hundred dollars; nine for the Indian service in the Territories of Arizona, Colorado, Idaho, Wyoming, and the State of Nevada, at five hundred dollars each; in all, forty thousand five hundred dollars.

For buildings at agencies, and repairs of same, ten thousand dollars.

For vaccine matter and vaccination of Indians, including deficiency, for current fiscal year, five thousand dollars.

For presents to and provisions for Indians, ten thousand dollars.

For the manufacture of medals for Indians, five thousand dollars.

For actual necessary expenses incurred, and that may hereafter be incurred, by officers of the Indian department, in the rescue of prisoners from Indian tribes and returning them to their homes, and for expenses incident to the arrest and confinement within the territory of the United States, by order of such officers, of persons charged with crimes against the Indians, five thousand dollars.

For contingencies, including travelling, incidental, current, and contingent of superintendents and agents, and of their offices, thirty-eight thousand five hundred dollars.

Apaches, Kiowas, and Comanches.—For fourth of thirty instalments, as provided to be expended under the tenth article of the treaty of October twenty-one, eighteen hundred and sixty-seven, concluded at Medicine Lodge Creek, in Kansas, with the Kiowas and Comanches, and under the third article of the treaty of same date with the Apaches, thirty thousand dollars.

For purchase of clothing, as provided in the same treaties, twenty-six thousand dollars.

For pay of carpenter, farmer, blacksmith, miller, and engineer, five thousand two hundred dollars.

For pay of physician and teacher, two thousand five hundred dollars.

For last of three instalments, as provided in the same treaties, to be expanded in presents to the ten persons of the said tribes who, in the judgment of the agent, may grow the most valuable crops for the period named, five hundred dollars.

For transportation of goods, five thousand dollars.

For purchase of seeds and agricultural implements to be furnished each head of a family or lodge who intends to commence cultivating the soil, (say one hundred families), ten thousand dollars.

Apaches of Arizona and Mexico.—For this amount, to be expended under the direction of the President, in collecting the Apaches of Arizona and New Mexico upon reservations, furnishing them with subsistence and other necessary articles, and to promote peace and civilization among them, seventy thousand dollars: *Provided*, That this appropriation shall be expended only in behalf of those Indians who go and remain upon said reservations, and refrain from hostilities.

Arickarees, Gros Ventres, and Mandas.—For this amount, to be expended in such goods, provisions, and other articles as the President may from time' to time determine, including insurance and transportation thereof, in instructing in agricultural and mechanical pursuits, in providing employees, educating children, procuring medicine and medical attendance, care for and support of the aged, sick, and infirm, for the helpless orphans of said Indians, and in any other respect to promote their civilization, comfort, and improvement, forty thousand dollars.

Assinaboines.—For this amount, to be expended in such goods, provisions, and other articles as the President may from time to time determine, including insurance and transportation thereof, in instructing in agricultural and mechanical pursuits, in providing employees, educating children, procuring medicine and medical attendance, care for and support of the aged, sick, and infirm, for the helpless orphans of said Indians, and in any other respect to promote their comfort, and improvement, thirty thousand dollars.

Blackfeet, Bloods, and Piegans.—For this amount, to be expended in Pam, such goods, provisions, and other articles as the President may from time to time determine, including insurance and transportation thereof, in instructing in agricultural and mechanical pursuits, in providing employees, educating children, procuring medicine and medical attendance, care for and support of the aged, nick, and infirm, for the helpless orphans of said Indians, and in every other respect to promote their civilization, comfort, and improvement; fifty thousand dollars.

Calapooias, Molallas, and Clackamas of Willamette Valley.—For of second of five instalments of the fourth series of annuity for beneficial objects, five thousand five hundred dollars.

Cheyenne and Arapahoes.—For fourth of thirty instalments provided to be expended under tenth article treaty October twenty-eight, eighteen hundred and sixty-seven, twenty thousand dollars.

For purchase of clothing, as per same article, fourteen thousand five hundred dollars.

For pay of physician and teacher, as per thirteenth article same treaty, two thousand five hundred dollars.

For pay of carpenter, farmer, blacksmith, miller, and engineer, as per same article, five thousand two hundred dollars.

For purchase of seeds and agricultural implements, to be furnished each head of a family or lodge, ten thousand dollars.

For last of three instalments, to be expended in presents to the ten persons of said tribe who, in the judgment of the agent, may grow the most valuable crops for the respective year, as per fourteenth article same treaty, five hundred dollars.

For transportation of goods, seven thousand five hundred dollars.

Chickasaws.—For permanent annuity in goods, three thousand dollars.

Boise Fort Band of Chippewas.—For sixth of twenty instalments, for the support of one blacksmith and assistant, and for tools, iron and steel, and other articles necessary for the blacksmith shop, as per third article treaty of April seventh, eighteen hundred and sixty-six, one thousand five hundred dollars.

For sixth of twenty instalments for the support of one schoolteacher, and for necessary books and stationery, as per third article treaty of April, seventh, eighteen hundred and sixty-six, eight hundred dollars.

For sixth of twenty instalments for the instruction of Indians in farming, and purchase of seeds, tools, and so forth, as per third article of treaty of April seventh, eighteen hundred and sixty-six, eight hundred dollars.

For sixth of twenty instalments of annuity in money, to be paid per capita, as per third article treaty of April seventh, eighteen hundred and sixty-six, three thousand five hundred dollars.

For sixth of twenty instalments of annuity in provisions, ammunition, and tobacco, as per third article treaty of April seventh, eighteen hundred and sixty-six, one thousand dollars.

For sixth of twenty instalments of annuity in goods and other articles, as per third article treaty of April seventh, eighteen hundred and sixty-six, six thousand five hundred dollars.

For transportation and necessary cost of delivery of annuity goods and provisions, per sixth article treaty of April seventh, eighteen hundred and sixty-six, one thousand five hundred dollars.

Chippewas of Lake Superior.—For seventeenth of twenty instalments in coin, per fourth article treaty thirtieth September, eighteen hundred and fifty-four, five thousand dollars.

For seventeenth of twenty instalments in goods, household furniture, and cooking utensils, per fourth article treaty thirtieth September, eighteen hundred and fifty-four, eight thousand dollars.

For seventeenth of twenty instalments for agricultural implements and cattle, carpenters' and other tools, and building materials, per fourth article treaty thirtieth September, eighteen hundred and fifty four, three thousand dollars.

For seventeenth of twenty instalments for moral and educational purposes, three hundred dollars of which to be paid to the Grand Portage band yearly, to enable them to maintain a school at their village, per fourth article treaty thirtieth September, eighteen hundred and fifty-four, three thousand dollars.

For seventeenth of twenty instalments for six smiths and assistants, per second and fifth articles treaty thirtieth September, eighteen hundred and fifty-four, five thousand and forty dollars.

For seventeenth of twenty instalments for the support of six smiths' shops, per second and fifth articles treaty thirtieth September, eighteen hundred and fifty-four, one thousand three hundred and twenty dollars.

For fifteenth of twenty instalments for the seventh smith and assistant, and support of shops, per second and fifth articles treaty thirtieth September, eighteen hundred and fifty-four, one thousand and sixty dollars.

For support of smith and shop, during the pleasure of the President, as per seventh and twelfth articles of treaty of April seventh, eighteen hundred and sixty-six, six hundred dollars.

For support of two farmers, during the pleasure of the President, as per twelfth article treaty of September thirtieth, eighteen hundred and fifty-four, and seventh article of treaty of April seventh, eighteen hundred and sixty-six, twelve hundred dollars.

For insurance, transportation, and necessary cost of delivery of annuity and provisions for Chippewas of Lake Superior, three thousand dollars.

For this amount, or so much thereof as may be necessary, to be used at the discretion of the President, to carry on the work of instructing and aiding the Chippewas of Lake Superior, including the Boise Fort band, in the arts of civilization, with a view to their self-support, fifteen thousand dollars.

Chippewas of the Mississippi.—For fifth of ten instalments of the of second series in money, per fourth article treaty fourth October, eighteen hundred and forty-two, and eighth article treaty thirtieth September, eighteen hundred and fifty-four, and third article treaty seventh May, eighteen hundred and sixty-four, four thousand one hundred and sixty-six dollars and sixty-seven cents.

For fifth of ten instalments of the second series, for the pay of two carpenters, per fourth article treaty fourth October, eighteen hundred and forty-two, and eighth article treaty thirtieth September, eighteen hundred and fifty-four, and third article treaty seventh May, eighteen hundred and sixty-four, four hundred dollars.

For fifth of ten instalments of the second series in goods, per fourth article treaty fourth October, eighteen hundred and forty-two, and eighth article treaty thirtieth September, eighteen hundred and fifty-four, and third article treaty seventh May, eighteen hundred and sixty-four, three thousand five hundred dollars.

For fifth of ten instalments of the second series, for support of schools, per fourth article treaty fourth October, eighteen hundred and forty-two, and eighth article treaty thirtieth September, eighteen hundred and fifty-four, and third article treaty seventh May, eighteen hundred and sixty-four, six hundred and sixty-six dollars and sixty-seven cents.

For fifth of ten instalments of second series, for the purchase of provisions and tobacco, per fourth article treaty fourth October, eighteen hundred and forty-two, and eighth article treaty thirtieth September, eighteen hundred and fifty-four, and third article of treaty seventh May, eighteen hundred and sixty-four, six hundred and sixty-seven dollars and sixty-seven cents.

For fifth of ten instalments of the second series, for the support of two smiths' shops, including the pay of two smiths and assistants, and furnishing iron and steel, per fourth article treaty fourth October, eighteen hundred and forty-two, and eighth article treaty thirtieth September, eighteen hundred and fifty four, and third article treaty of seventh May, eighteen hundred and sixty-four, six hundred and sixty-seven dollars and sixty-seven cents.

For fifth of ten instalments of the second series, for pay of two farmers, per third article treaty May seventh, eighteen hundred and sixty-four, three hundred and thirty-three dollars and thirty-three cents.

For seventeenth of twenty instalments of annuity in money, per third article treaty of twenty-second February, eighteen hundred and fifty-five, twenty thousand dollars.

For twenty-fifth of twenty-six instalments, to be paid the Chippewas of Mississippi, per third article treaty of August second, eighteen hundred and forty-seven, one thousand dollars.

For fourth of ten instalments, for the support of a school or schools upon said reservation, in accordance with third article of treaty of March nineteenth, eighteen hundred and sixty-seven, four thousand dollars.

For fourth of ten instalments, to be expended in promoting the progress of the people in agriculture and assisting them to become self-sustaining, in accordance with third article of treaty of March nineteenth, eighteen hundred and sixty-seven, six thousand dollars.

For fourth of ten instalments, for the support of a physician, in accordance with third article treaty of March nineteen, eighteen hundred and sixty-seven, one thousand two hundred dollars.

For fourth of ten instalments, for the purchase of necessary medicines, in accordance with third article of treaty March nineteen, eighteen hundred and sixty-seven, three hundred dollars.

For insurance, transportation, and necessary cost of delivery of annuities and provisions for Chippewas of Mississippi, in accordance with sixth article of the treaty of March nineteen, eighteen hundred and sixty-seven, one thousand five hundred dollars.

Chippewas of the Mississippi, Pillager, and Lab Winnebag(o)shish Bands of Chippewa Indians.—For eighth of ten instalments to furnish said Indians with ten yoke of good work-oxen, twenty log-chains, two hundred grubbing hoes, ten plows, ten grindstones, one hundred axes, hash bands of (handled), twenty spades, and other farming implements, per fifth article treaty May seventh, eighteen hundred and sixty-four, one thousand five hundred dollars.

For the pay of two carpenters, one thousand eight hundred dollars, and two blacksmiths, one thousand eight hundred dollars; four farm laborers, two thousand four hundred dollars; one physician, one thousand two hundred dollars; and medicine for the sick, five hundred dollars, per fifth article treaty May seventh, eighteen hundred and sixty-four, seven thousand seven hundred dollars.

For this amount, to be applied toward the support of a saw-mill, to be built for the common use of the Chippewas of the Mississippi and the Red Lake and Pembina bands of Chippewas, as per sixth article treaty of May seventh, eighteen hundred and sixty-four, one thousand dollars.

For pay of services and travelling expenses of a board of visitors, to consist of not more than three persons, to attend the annuity payments to the Indians, and to inspect the fields, buildings, mills, and other improvements, as stipulated in the seventh article treaty May seventh, eighteen hundred and sixty-four, not exceeding anyone year more than twenty days' service, at five dollars per day, or more than three hundred miles' travel, at ten cents per mile, four hundred and eighty dollars.

For pay of female teachers employed on the reservations to instruct Indian girls in domestic economy, one thousand dollars.

Chippewas, Pillager, and Lake Winnebagoshish Bands.—For seventeenth of thirty instalments of annuity in money, per third article treaty twenty-second February, eighteen hundred and fifty-five, ten thousand six hundred and sixty-six dollars and sixty-six cents.

For seventeenth of thirty instalments of annuity in goods, per third article treaty twenty-second February, eighteen hundred and fifty-five, eight thousand dollars.

For seventeenth of thirty instalments for purposes of utility, per third article treaty twenty-second February, eighteen hundred and fifty-five, four thousand dollars.

For seventeenth of twenty instalments for purposes of education, per third article treaty twenty-second February, eighteen hundred and fifty-five, three thousand dollars.

Chippewas of Red Lake and Pembina Tribe of Chippewas.—For this Chippewes of amount as annuity to be paid per capita to the like band of Chippewas during the pleasure of the President, per third article treaty second October, eighteen hundred and sixty-three, and second article supplementary to treaty April twelve, eighteen hundred and sixty-four, ten thousand dollars.

For this amount, to the Pembina band of Chippewas, during the pleasure of the President, per same treaty, five thousand dollars.

For eighth of fifteen instalments for the purpose of supplying the Red take band of Chippewas with gilling twine, cotton matter, calico; linsey, blankets, sheeting, flannels, provisions, farming tools, and for such other useful articles and for such other useful purposes as may be deemed for their best interests, per third article supplementary treaty of twelfth April, eighteen hundred and sixty-four, eight thousand dollars.

For eighth of fifteen instalments for same objects for Pembina band o Chippewas, per same treaty, four thousand dollars.

For eighth of fifteen instalments for pay of one blacksmith, one physician, who shall furnish medicine for the sick, one miller, and one farmer, per fourth article of same treaty, three thousand nine hundred dollars.

For eighth of fifteen instalments for the purchase of iron and steel, and other articles, for blacksmithing purposes, per same treaty as above, one thousand five hundred dollars.

For eighth of fifteen instalments, to be expended for carpentering, and other purposes, per same treaty, one thousand dollars.

For eighth of fifteen instalments, to defray expenses of a board of visitors, to consist of not more than three persons, to attend the annuity payments of the said Chippewa Indians; each member of the board to be paid not more than five dollars per day, for not more than twenty days' service, and ten cents per mile for not more than three hundred mile travel, three hundred and ninety dollars.

For insurance and transportation of annuity goods and provisions, and iron and steel for blacksmiths, for the Chippewas of Red Lake and Pembina tribe, three thousand dollars.

For this amount or so much thereof as may be necessary, to be used at the discretion of the President, to carry on the work of instructing and aiding the Chippewas of Red Lake, the Pembina tribe of Chippewas, and other Indians of the Mississippi Chippewa agency, (not including the Chippewas of Lake Superior), in the arts of civilization, with a view to their self-support, twenty thousand dollars.

Choctaws.—For permanent annuity, per second article treaty sixteenth November, eighteen hundred and five, and thirteenth article treaty twenty-second June, eighteen hundred and fifty-five, three thousand dollars.

For permanent annul ty for support of light-horsemen, per thirteenth article treaty eighteenth October, eighteen hundred and twenty, and article thirteen, treaty twenty-second dune, eighteen hundred and fifty-five, six hundred dollars.

For permanent annuity for support of blacksmith, per sixth article treaty eighteenth October, eighteen hundred and twenty, ninth article treaty January twenty, eighteen hundred and twenty-five, and thirteenth article treaty twenty-second June, eighteen hundred and fifty-five, six hundred dollars.

For permanent annuity for education, per second article treaty twentieth January, eighteen hundred and twenty-five, and thirteenth article treaty twenty-second June, eighteen hundred and fifty-five, six thousand dollars.

For permanent annuity of iron and steel, per ninth article treaty twentieth January, eighteen hundred and twenty-five, and thirteenth article of treaty twenty-second June, eighteen hundred and fifty-five, three hundred and twenty dollars.

For interest on three hundred and ninety thousand two hundred and fifty-seven dollars and ninety-two cents, at five per centum per annum, for education, support of the government, and other beneficial purposes, under the direction of the general council of the Choctaws, in conformity with the provisions contained in the ninth and thirteenth articles of the treaty twentieth January, eighteen hundred and twenty-five, and treaty of twenty-second of June, eighteen hundred and fifty-five, nineteen thousand five hundred and twelve dollars and eighty-nine cents.

Confederated Tribes and Bands of Indians in Middle Oregon.— For second of five instalments, third series, for beneficial objects, per second article treaty twenty-fifth June, eighteen hundred and fifty-five, four thousand dollars.

For twelfth of fifteen instalments for pay and subsistence of one farmer, one blacksmith, and one wagon and plow-maker, per fourth article treaty twenty-fifth of June, eighteen hundred and fifty-five, three thousand five hundred dollars.

For twelfth of twenty instalments for pay and subsistence of one physician, one sawyer, one miller, one superintendent of farming operations, and one school-teacher, per fourth article treaty twenty-fifth June, eighteen hundred and fifty-five, five thousand six hundred dollars.

For twelfth of twenty installments for salary of the head chief of said confederated bands, per fourth article treaty twenty-fifth June, eighteen hundred and fifty-five, five hundred dollars.

Creeks.—For permanent annuity in money, per fourth article treaty Creeks seventh August, seventeen hundred and ninety, and fifth article treaty seventh August, eighteen hundred and fifty-six, one thousand five hundred dollars.

For permanent annuity in money, per second article treaty sixteenth June, eighteen hundred and two, and fifth article treaty seventh August, eighteen hundred and fifty-six, three thousand dollars.

For permanent annuity in money, per fourth article treat twenty-fourth January, eighteen hundred and twenty-six, and fifth article treaty seventh August, eighteen hundred and fifty-six, twenty thousand dollars.

For permanent annuity for blacksmith and assistant, and for shop and tools, per eighth article treaty twenty-fourth January, eighteen hundred and twenty-six, and fifth article treaty seventh August, eighteen hundred and fifty-six, eight hundred and forty dollars.

For permanent annuity for iron and steel for shop, per eighth article treaty twenty-fourth January, eighteen hundred and twenty-six, and fifth article treaty seventh August, eighteen hundred aql fifty-six, two hundred and seventy dollars.

For permanent annuity for the pay of a wheelwright, per eighth article treaty twenty-fourth January, eighteen hundred and twenty-six, and fifth article treaty seventh August, eighteen hundred and fifty-six, six hundred dollars.

For blacksmith and assistant, shop and tools, eight hundred and forty dollars.

For iron and steel of shop, three hundred and seventy dollars.

For wagon-maker, six hundred dollars.

For education, one thousand dollars.

For assistance in agricultural operations, two thousand dollars.

For five per centum interest on two hundred thousand dollars, for purposes of education, per sixth article treaty seventh August, eighteen hundred and fifty-six, ten thousand dollars.

For interest on six hundred and seventy-five thousand one hundred and sixty-eight dollars, at the rate of five per centum per annum, to be expended under the direction of the Secretary of the Interior, under provisions of third article treaty June fourteen, eighteen hundred and sixty-six, thirty-three thousand seven hundred and fifty-eight dollars and forty cents.

Crows.—For third of thirty instalments to supply male persons, six hundred in number, over fourteen years of age, with a suit of good substantial woollen clothing, consisting of coat, hat, pantaloons, flannel shirt, and woolen socks, as per ninth article of treaty of May seven, eighteen hundred and sixty-eight, eight thousand four hundred dollars.

For third of thirty instalments to supply each female, seven hundred in number, over twelve years of age, with a flannel shirt, or the goods necessary to make the same, a pair of woolen hose, twelve yards of calico, and twelve yards of cotton domestic, as per same article, eight thousand four hundred dollars.

For third of thirty instalments to supply three hundred and fifty boys and three hundred and fifty girls, under the ages named, such flannel and cotton goods as may be needed to make each a suit as aforesaid, together with a pair of woolen hose for each, as per same article, five thousand nine hundred and twenty-three dollars.

For third of ten instalments, to be used by the Secretary of the Interior in the purchase of such articles as from time to time the condition and necessities may indicate to be proper, the sum of ten dollars for each Indian roaming, as per same article, a sum not exceeding five thousand dollars.

For pay of a physician, one thousand four hundred dollars.

For second of twenty instalments for pay of teacher and furnishing necessary books and stationery, under seventh article same treaty, three thousand dollars.

For first of three instalments for the purchase of seeds and implements for such Indians as shall continue to farm, (say fifty souls), one thousand two hundred and fifty dollars.

For pay of second blacksmith, iron and steel, as per eighth article same treaty, two thousand dollars.

For second of ten instalments, to be used by the Secretary of the Interior in the purchase of such articles as from time to time the condition and necessities of the Indians may indicate to be proper, the sum of twenty dollars for each Indian engaged in agriculture, as per ninth article of the same treaty, a sum not exceeding twenty thousand dollars.

For second of four instalments to furnish said Indians with flour and meat, as per ninth article treaty May seven, eighteen hundred and sixty eight, one hundred and thirty-one thousand four hundred dollars.

For second of three instalments, to be expended in presents to the ten persons of said tribe who, in the judgment of the agent, may grow the most valuable crops, as per twelfth article same treaty, five hundred dollars.

For pay of carpenter, miller, engineer, farmer, and blacksmith, as per fifteenth article of same treaty, five thousand two hundred dollars.

For insurance and transportation of goods, eight thousand dollars.

Delawares.—For life annuity to chief, per private article to supplemental treaty twenty-fourth September, eighteen hundred and twenty nine, to treaty of third October, eighteen hundred and eighteen, one hundred dollars: *Provided*, That satisfactory evidence shall be shown to the Secretary of the Interior that the chi provided for by said private article is still alive.

For interest on forty-six thousand and eighty dollars, at five per centum, being the value of thirty-six sections of land set apart by treaty of eighteen hundred and twenty-nine for education, per Senate resolution June thirteen, eighteen hundred and thirty-nine, and fifth article treaty of May sixth, eighteen hundred and fifty-six (four), two thousand three hundred and four dollars.

D' Wamisk and other allied tribes in Washington Territory.—For twelfth instalment on one hundred and fifty thousand dollars, under the direction of the President, per sixth article treaty twenty-second January, eighteen hundred fifty-five, six thousand dollars.

For twelfth of twenty instalments for the establishment and support of an agricultural and industrial school, and to provide said school with a suitable instructor or instructors, per fourteenth article treaty twenty second January, eighteen hundred and fifty-five, three thousand dollars.

For twelfth of twenty instalments for the support of a smith and carpenter shop, and furnishing it with necessary tools, five hundred dollars.

For twelfth of twenty instalments for the employment of a blacksmith, carpenter, farmer, and physician, who shall furnish medicines for the sick, per fourteenth article treaty twenty-second January, eighteen hundred and fifty-five, four thousand six hundred dollars.

Flatheads and other Confederated Tribes.—For the third of five instalments on one hundred and twenty thousand dollars, being the third series, for beneficial objects, at the discretion of the President, per fourth article treaty sixteenth July, eighteen hundred and fifty-five, four thousand dollars.

For twelfth of twenty instalments for the support of an agricultural and industrial school, keeping in repair the buildings, and providing suitable furniture, books, and stationery, per fifth article treaty sixteenth July, eighteen hundred and fifty-five, three hundred dollars.

For twelfth of twenty instalments for providing suitable instructors therefor, per fifth article treaty sixteenth July, eighteen hundred and fifty-five, one thousand eight hundred dollars.

For twelfth of twenty instalments for keeping in repair blacksmiths', tin and gunsmiths', carpenters', and wagon and plow makers' shops and providing necessary tools therefor, per fifth article treaty sixteenth July, eighteen hundred and fifty-five, five hundred dollars.

For twelfth of twenty instalments for the employment of two farmers, two millers, one blacksmith, one tinner, one gunsmith, one carpenter, and one wagon and plow maker, per fifth article treaty sixteenth July, eighteen hundred and fifty-five, seven thousand four hundred dollars.

For twelfth of twenty instalments for keeping in repair saw and flouring mills, and for furnishing the necessary tools and fixtures therefor, per fifth article treaty sixteenth July, eighteen hundred and fifty-five, five hundred dollars.

For twelfth of twenty instalments for keeping in repair the hospital and providing the necessary medicines and furniture therefor, per fifth article treaty sixteenth July, eighteen-hundred and fifty-five, three hundred dollars.

For twelfth of twenty instalments for pay of a physician, per fifth article treaty sixteenth duly, eighteen hundred and fifty-five, one thousand four hundred dollars.

For twelfth of twenty instalments for keeping in repair the buildings required for the various employees, and furnishing the necessary furniture therefor, per fifth article treaty sixteenth July, eighteen hundred and fifty-five, three hundred dollars.

For twelfth of twenty instalments for the pay of each of the head chiefs of the Flathead, Kootenay, and Upper Pend d'Oreilles tribes, per fifth article treaty sixteenth July, eighteen hundred and fifty five, one thousand five hundred dollars.

For insurance and transportation of annuity goods and provisions to said Indians, per fifth article treaty of July sixteenth, eighteen hundred and fifty-five, two thousand dollars.

Gros Ventres.—For this amount, to be expended in such goods, provisions, and other articles as the President may from time to time determine, including insurance and transportation thereof, in instructing in agricultural and mechanical pursuits, in providing employees, educating children, procuring medicine and medical attendance, care for and support of the aged, sick, and infirm, for the helpless orphans of said Indians, and in any other respect to promote their civilization, comfort, and improvement, thirty-five thousand dollars.

Iowas.—For interest in lien of investment on fifty-seven thousand five hundred dollars, balance of one hundred and fifty-seven thousand five hundred dollars, to the first of July, eighteen hundred and seventy-one, at five per centum per annum, for education or other beneficial purposes, under the direction of the President, ninth article of treaty of May seventeen, eighteen hundred and fifty, two thousand eight hundred and seventy-five dollars.

Kansas.—For interest in lien of investment on two hundred thousand dollars, at five per centum per annum, per second article treaty of January fourteen, eighteen hundred and forty-six, ten thousand dollars.

Kickapoos.—For eighteenth instalment of interest on one hundred thousand dollars, at five per centum per annum, for educational and other beneficial purposes, per treaty of May eighteen, eighteen hundred and fifty-four, five thousand dollars.

For eighteenth instalment on two hundred thousand dollars, to be paid in eighteen hundred and seventy-two, per second article treaty eighteenth May, eighteen hundred and fifty-four, five thousand dollars.

Klamath and Modoc Indians.—For the first of five instalments, to be applied under direction of the President, as per second article treaty of October fourteen, eighteen hundred and sixty-four, five thousand dollars.

For fifth of twenty instalments for keeping in repair one saw-mill, one flouring-mill, buildings for the blacksmith, carpenter, and wagon and plow maker, the manual-labor school, and hospital, as per fourth article treaty of October fourteen, eighteen hundred and sixty-four, one thousand dollars.

For sixth of twenty instalments, for the purchase of tools and material for saw and flour mills, carpenter, blacksmith, wagon and plow maker's shops, and books and stationery for the manual-labor school, as per fourth article treaty of October fourteen, eighteen hundred and sixty-four, one thousand five hundred dollars.

For sixth of fifteen instalments, for pay and, subsistence of one superintendent of farming, one farmer, one blacksmith, one sawyer, one carpenter, and one wagon and plow maker, as per fifth article treaty of October fourteen, eighteen hundred and sixty-four, six thousand dollars.

For sixth of twenty instalments to pay salary and subsistence of one physician, one miller, and two school-teachers, as per fifth article treaty of October fourteen, eighteen hundred and sixty-four, three thousand six hundred dollars.

Makda Tribe.—For second of ten instalments of thirty thousand dollars (being the fifth series), under direction of the President, as per fifth article of treaty of January thirty-one, eighteen hundred and five, one thousand dollars.

For twelfth of twenty instalments for support of a smith and carpenter's shop, and to provide the necessary tools therefor, per eleventh article treaty thirty-first January, eighteen hundred and fifty-five, five hundred dollars.

For twelfth of twenty instalments for the support of an agricultural and industrial school, and pay of teachers, two thousand five hundred dollars.

For twelfth of twenty instalments for the employment of a blacksmith, carpenter, farmer, and physician, who shall furnish medicine for the sick, four thousand six hundred dollars.

Meaomonees.—For sixth of fifteen instalments of annuity upon two hundred and forty-two thousand six hundred and eighty-six dollars, for cession of lands, per fourth article treaty May twelve, eighteen hundred and fifty-four, and Senate amendment thereto, sixteen thousand one hundred and seventy-nine dollars and six cents.

Miamies of Kansas.—For permanent provision for blacksmith and assistant, and iron and steel for shop, per fifth article treaty sixth October, eighteen hundred and eighteen, and fourth article treaty June five, eighteen hundred and fifty-four, nine hundred and forty dollars.

For permanent provision for miller, in lieu of gunsmith, per fifth article treaty sixth October, eighteen hundred and eighteen, fifth article treaty twenty-third October, eighteen hundred and thirty-four, and fourth article treaty fifth June, eighteen hundred and fifty-four, six hundred dollars

For interest on fifty thousand dollars, at five per contain, for educational purposes, per third article treaty fifth June, eighteen hundred and fifty-four, two thousand five hundred dollars.

For twelfth of twenty instalments upon two hundred thousand dollars, per third article treaty fifth June, eighteen hundred and fifty-four, seven thousand five hundred dollars.

Miamies—Eel River.—For permanent annuity in goods or otherwise, per fourth article treaty third August, seventeen hundred and ninety five, five hundred dollars.

For permanent annuity in goods or otherwise, per articles treaty twenty-first August, eighteen hundred and five, two hundred and fifty dollars.

For permanent annuity in goods or otherwise, per third and separate articles of treaty of thirtieth September, eighteen hundred and nine, three hundred and fifty dollars.

Miamies of Indiana.—For interest on two hundred and twenty-one thousand two hundred and fifty-seven dollars and eighty-six cents uninvested, at five per centum, per Senate amendment to fourth article treaty fifth June, eighteen hundred and fifty-four, eleven thousand and sixty-two dollars and eighty-nine cents.

Molels.—For pay of teachers of manual-labor schools, for all necessary materials therefor, and for the subsistence of the pupils, two thousand dollars.

Mixed Shoshones, Bannocks, and Sheepeaters.—For this amount to be expended in such goods, provisions, an articles as the President may from time to time determine, including insurance and transportation thereof, in instructing in agricultural and mechanical pursuits, in providing employees, educating children, procuring medicine and medical attendance, care for and support of the aged, sick, and infirm, for the helpless orphans of said Indians, and in any other respect to promote their civilzation, comfort, and improvement, twenty-five thousand dollars.

Navajoes.—For third of ten instalments of such articles of clothing, or raw material in lieu thereof, for eight thousand Navajoe Indians, not exceeding five dollars per Indian, as per eighth article of treaty of June one, eighteen hundred and sixty-eight, forty thousand dollars.

For last of three instalments for seeds and agricultural implements for fourteen hundred families, at the rate of twenty-five dollars per family, as per seventh article same treaty, thirty-five thousand dollars.

For second of ten instalments to be used by the commissioner of Indian affairs in the purchase of such articles as from time to time the condition and necessities of the Indians may indicate to be proper, the sum of ten dollars to each person who engages in farming or mechanical pursuits, (one thousand four hundred families), as per eighth article of the same treaty, fourteen thousand dollars.

For pay of two teachers, two thousand dollars.

For insurance and transportation of goods, fifteen thousand dollars.

Nez Perces Indians.—For second of five instalments of third series for beneficial objects, at the discretion of the President, per fourth article treaty of June eleven, eighteen hundred and fifty-five, six thousand dollars.

For twelfth of twenty instalments for the support of two schools, one of which to be an- agricultural and industrial school, keeping in repair school buildings, and for providing suitable furniture, books, and stationery, per fifth article treaty June eleven, eighteen hundred and fifty five, five hundred dollars.

For twelfth of twenty instalments for the employment of one superintendent of teaching, and two teachers, per fifth article treaty June eleven, eighteen hundred and fifty five, three thousand two hundred dollars.

For twelfth of twenty instalments for the employment of one superintendent of farming, and two farmers, two millers, two blacksmiths, one tanner, one gunsmith, one carpenter, and one wagon and plow maker, per fifth article treaty eleventh of June, eighteen hundred and fifty-five, ten thousand dollars.

For twelfth of twenty instalments for pay of a physician, per fifth article treaty eleventh June, eighteen hundred and fifty-five, one thousand four hundred dollars.

For twelfth of twenty instalments for keeping in repair the buildings for the various employees, and for providing the necessary furniture therefor, per fifth article treaty eleventh June, eighteen hundred and fifty-five, three hundred dollars.

For twelfth of twenty instalments for the salary of such person as the tribe may select to be their head chief, per fifth article treaty eleventh June, eighteen hundred and fifty-five, five hundred dollars.

For salary of two subordinate chiefs, as per fifth article treaty of June nine, eighteen hundred and sixty-three, one thousand dollars.

For sixth of sixteen instalments for boarding and clothing the children who shall attend the schools, providing the schools and boarding-houses with necessary furniture, the purchase of necessary wagons, teams, agricultural implements, tools, and so forth, and for fencing of such lands as may be needed for gardening and farming purposes for the schools, three thousand dollars.

For salary of two matrons to take charge of the boarding-schools, two assistant teachers, one farmer, one carpenter, and two millers, seven thousand six hundred dollars.

For twelfth of twenty instalments for keeping in repair the hospital, and providing the necessary medicines, and the furniture therefor, three hundred dollars.

For repairs of houses, mills, and tools, and necessary materials, three thousand five hundred dollars.

Nisqually, Puyallup, and other Tribes and Bands of Indians.—For seventeenth instalment, in part payment for relinquishment of title to lands, to be applied to beneficial objects, per fourth article treaty twenty-sixth December, eighteen hundred and fifty-four, one thousand dollars.

For seventeenth of twenty instalments for pay of instructors, smith, carpenter, farmer, and physician, who shall furnish medicine to the sick, per tenth article treaty twenty-sixth December, eighteen hundred and fifty-four, six thousand seven hundred dollars.

For seventeenth of twenty instalments for the support of an agricultural and industrial school, and support of smith and carpenter shop, and providing the 'necessary tools therefor, in conformity with tenth article of the treaty of December twenty-six, eighteen hundred and fifty-four, one thousand five hundred dollars.

Northern Oheynnes and Arapahoes.—For third of thirty instalments for purchase of clothing, as per sixth article of treaty of May ten, eighteen hundred and sixty-eight, fifteen thousand dollars.

For third of ten instalments, to be expended by the Secretary of the. Interior, ten dollars for each Indian roaming, (one thousand eight hundred souls), in the purchase of such articles as from time to time the condition and necessities of the Indiana may indicate to be proper, as per same treaty, eighteen thousand dollars.

For third of four instalments, as per same treaty, to furnish said Indians flour and meat, sixty-six thousand five hundred and seventy-six dollars.

For pay of physician, teacher, carpenter, miller, farmer, blacksmith, and engineer, seven thousand seven hundred dollars.

For last of three instalments, to be expended in presents to the ten persons of said tribe who, in the judgment of the agent, may grow the most valuable crops for the respective year, five hundred dollars.

For insurance and transportation of goods, six thousand dollars.

Omahas.—For the fourth of fifteen instalments of this amount, being third series, in money or otherwise, per fourth article treaty sixteenth March, eighteen hundred and fifty-four, twenty thousand dollars.

For sixth of ten instalments for keeping in repair a grist and saw mill, and support of blacksmith shop per eighth article treaty March sixteenth, eighteen hundred and fifty-four, and third article treaty March six, eighteen hundred and sixty-five, three hundred dollars.

For sixth of ten instalments for pay of one engineer, one thousand two handrail dollars.

For sixth of ten instalments for pay of one miller, per same treaties, nine hundred dollars.

For sixth of ten instalments for pay of one farmer, per same treaties, nine hundred dollars.

For sixth of ten instalments for pay of blacksmith, per same treaties, nine hundred dollars.

For fourth of ten instalments for support of blacksmith shop, and supplying tools for the same, three hundred dollars.

Osages.—For interest on sixty-nine thousand one hundred and twenty dollars, at five per centum per annum, being value of fifty-four sections ¢ land set apart by treaty of June two, eighteen hundred and twenty-five, for educational purposes, per Senate resolution of January nine, eighteen hundred and thirty-eight, three thousand four hundred and fifty-six dollars.

For interest on three hundred thousand dollars, at five per centum per annum, to be paid semi-annually, in money or such articles as the Secretary of the Interior may direct, as per first article treaty of September twenty-nine, eighteen hundred and sixty-five, fifteen thousand dollars: *Provided*, That each half-breed or mixed-blood of the Osages, being certain twenty-one years of age, or the head of a family, shall, under such rules and regulations and on such proofs as shall be prescribed by the Secretary of the Interior, be entitled to enter, without cost, within the diminished reservation of the Osage Indians in Kansas, a tract of land, in compact of form and by legal subdivisions, not exceeding one hundred and sixty acres, upon which such half-breed or mixed-blood have heretofore actually settled and made improvements: *Provided, however,* That such half-breed certain claim or mixed-blood so entering such land shall thereby forfeit all claim to lands within the Indian Territory which have been or shall be purchased out of the proceeds of the sale of the land of the Osages, in the State of Kansas: *And provided further,* That the land so entered shall not be alienable by such half-breed or mixed-blood without the consent of the Secretary of the Interior, approved by the President.

For the purpose of providing subsistence and clothing, and aiding said Indians in establishing themselves in their new homes, fifty thousand dollars, to be reimbursed to the United States from the interest on the proceeds of the sales of the lands of the said Indians in Kansas: *Provided*, That the laws of the United States relating to town sites be extended pup tended over all the lands obtained of the Osage Indians in the State of lands in Kansas.

Ottawas and Chippewas of Michigan.—For last of four equal instalments in coin of the sum of two hundred and six thousand dollars, being the unpaid part of the principal sum of three hundred and six thousand dollars, to be distributed per capita, in the usual manner of paying annuities, per third (second) article of the treaty of thirty-first July, eighteen hundred and fifty-five, fifty-one thousand five hundred dollars.

Ottoes and Missourias.—For fourth of fifteen instalments, being the third series, in money or otherwise, per fourth article treaty fifteenth March, eighteen hundred and fifty-four, nine thousand dollars.

Pawnees.—For perpetual annuity, at least one half of which to be in goods and such articles as may be deemed necessary for them, per second article treaty twenty-fourth September, eighteen hundred and fifty-seven, thirty thousand dollars.

For support of two manual-labor schools, per third, article treaty September twenty-four, eighteen hundred and fifty-seven, ten thousand dollars.

For pay of one farmer, two blacksmiths, and two apprentices, one miller and apprentice, one engineer, and two teachers, five thousand seven hundred and eighty dollars.

For pay of physician and purchase of medicines, one thousand dollars.

For the purchase of iron and steel and other necessaries for the shops, five hundred dollars.

For the purchase of farming utensils and stock, twelve hundred dollars.

For repair of grist and saw mills, three hundred dollars.

For transportation and insurance, and necessary cost of delivery of annuities for the Pawnees, two thousand dollars.

Poncas.—For eighth of ten instalments, (second series), to be paid to them or expended for their benefit, ten thousand dollars

For this amount to be expended during the pleasure of the President in furnishing such aid and assistance in agricultural and mechanical pursuits, including the working of the mill, as provided by second article of the treaty of March twelve, eighteen hundred and *sixty* (fifty)-eight, as the Secretary of the Interior may consider advantageous and necessary, seven thousand five hundred dollars.

For this amount, or so much thereof as, may be necessary, to be used at the discretion of the President, to carry on the work of aiding and instructing the Poncas in the arts of civilization, with a view to their self-support, and for subsistence and clothing, ten thousand dollars.

Pottawatomies.—For permanent annuity in silver, per fourth article treaty third August, seventeen hundred and ninety-five, four hundred and eighteen dollars and thirty-five cents.

For permanent annuity in silver, per third article treaty thirtieth September, eighteen hundred and nine, two hundred and nine dollars and eighteen cents.

For permanent annuity in silver, per third article treaty second October, eighteen hundred and eighteen, one thousand and forty-five dollars and eighty-seven cents.

For permanent annuity in money, per second article treaty twentieth September, eighteen hundred and twenty-eight, eight hundred and thirty-six dollars and sixty-nine cents.

For permanent annuity in specie, per second article treaty twenty-ninth July, eighteen hundred and twenty-nine, six thousand six hundred and ninety-three dollars and fifty-eight cents.

For life annuity to chief (Alexander Robinson), per third article treaty of October twenty, eighteen hundred and thirty-two, and third article treaty September twenty-six, eighteen hundred and thirty-three, five hundred dollars: *Provided*, That satisfactory evidence shall be shown to the Secretary of the Interior that the said chief provided for by said articles is still living.

For educational purposes, five thousand dollars.

For permanent provision for payment of money, in lieu of tobacco, iron, and steel, per second article treaty twentieth September, eighteen hundred and twenty-eight, and tenth article of the treaty of the fifth and seventeenth June, eighteen hundred and forty-six, one hundred and twenty-five dollars and fifty cents.

For permanent provisions for three blacksmiths and assistants, and for iron and steel for shops, per third article treaty sixteenth October, eighteen hundred and twenty-six, second article treaty twentieth September, eighteen hundred and twenty-eight, and second article treaty twenty-ninth July, eighteen hundred and twenty-nine, one thousand one hundred and seventy-nine dollars and seventy-four cents.

For permanent provision for flay barrels of salt, per second article of treaty twenty-ninth July, eighteen hundred and twenty-nine, one hundred and eighty-three dollars and three cents.

For interest on two hundred and sixty-eight thousand nine hundred and ninety-eight dollars and seventeen cents, at five per centum, in conformity with provisions of article seven of treaties of June five and seventeen, eighteen hundred and forty-six, thirteen thousand four hundred and forty-nine dollars and ninety cents.

For this amount to be charged to the Pottawatomie fund, to enable the President of the United States to carry out the provisions of the third article of the treaty of November fifteen, eighteen hundred and sixty-one, with the Pottawatomie Indians, as modified by the treaty of March twenty-nine, eighteen hundred and sixty-six, by paying to those two hundred and fifty members of the tribe who have elected to become citizens, in accordance with said article, the proportion of the cash value of the Pottawatomie annuities to which they are entitled, one hundred and thirty-two thousand three hundred and fifty-six dollars and sixty-five cents, or so much thereof as may be necessary to comply with the provisions of said treaties, of Which amount forty-five thousand eight hundred and seventy-one dollars and fifty-six cents, or so much thereof as may be necessary, is hereby appropriated in coin, as contemplated in treaties of November fifteen, eighteen hundred and sixty-one, and March twenty-nine, eighteen hundred and sixty-six. And the Secretary of the Interior is hereby authorized to sell two hundred and fifty twenty-one hundred-and-eightieth parts of the several classes of bonds originally held (before the distribution made to the six hundred Pottawatomies by act of July twenty-seven, eighteen hundred and sixty-eight) by him in trust for and belonging to said Pottawatomie Indians, and pay the proceeds thereof without any deduction, in compliance with the provisions of said treaties, it being the share of the above-mentioned two hundred and fifty persons in the bonds belonging to said Indians.

Pottawatomies of Huron.—For permanent annuity, in money or otherwise, per second article treaty of November seventeen, eighteen hundred and seven, four hundred dollars.

Quapaws.—For this amount, to be expended in such goods, provisions, we. and other articles as the President may from time to time determine, including insurance and transportation thereof, in instructing in agricultural and mechanical pursuits, in providing employees, educating children, procuring medicine and medical attendance, care for and support of the aged, sick, and infirm, for the helpless orphans of said Indians, and in any other respect to promote their civilization and improvement, two thousand six hundred and sixty dollars.

Qua-nai-elt and Qui-leh-ute Indians.—For the second of five instalments on twenty-five thousand dollars (being the first series) for beneficial objects, under the direction of the President, per fourth article treaty of July one, eighteen hundred and fifty-five, one thousand dollars

For twelfth of twenty instalments for the support of an agricultural and industrial school, and for pay of suitable instructors, per tenth article treaty July one, eighteen hundred and fifty-five, two thousand five hundred dollars.

For twelfth of twenty instalments for support of smith and carpenter shop, and to provide the necessary tools therefor, per tenth article treaty July one, eighteen hundred and fifty-five, five hundred dollars.

For twelfth of twenty instalments for-the employment of a blacksmith, carpenter, and farmer, and a physician, who shall furnish medicines for the sick, per tenth article treaty July one, eighteen hundred and fifty five, four thousand one hundred dollars.

River Crows.—For this amount, to be expended for such goods, provisions, and other articles as the President from time to time may determine, including insurance and transportation thereof, in instructing in agricultural and mechanical pursuits, in providing employees, educating children, procuring medicine and medical attendance, care for and support of the aged, sick, and infirm, for the helpless orphans of said Indiana, and in any other respect to promote their civilization, comfort, and improvement, thirty thousand dollars.

Rogue Rivers.—For second of five instalments in blankets, clothing, farming utensils, and stock, per third article treaty September ten, eighteen hundred and fifty-three, three thousand dollars.

Sans and Foxes of the Mississippi.—For permanent annuity in goods or otherwise, per third article treaty November three, eighteen hundred and four, one thousand dollars.

For interest on two hundred thousand dollars, at five per centum, per second article treaty October twenty-one, eighteen hundred and thirty seven, ten thousand dollars.

For interest on eight hundred thousand dollars, at five per contain, per second article treaty October eleven, eighteen hundred and forty-two, forty thousand dollars.

For third of five instalments for support of a physician and purchase of medicines, one thousand five hundred dollars.

For third of five instalments for supplying said tribes with tobacco and salt, three hundred and fifty dollars.

Sacs and Foxes of Missouri.—For interest on one hundred and fifty-seven thousand four hundred dollars, at five per centum, under the direction of the President, per second article treaty of October twenty-one, eighteen hundred and thirty-seven, seven thousand eight hundred and seventy dollars.

For interest on eleven thousand six hundred and fifteen dollars and twenty-five cents, at five per centum, from June seventeen, eighteen hundred and sixty-five, to January one, eighteen hundred and seventy, two thousand six hundred and thirty-six dollars and forty-nine cents.

Seminoles.—For five per centum interest on two hundred and fifty thousand dollars, to be paid as annuity, per eighth article treaty August seven, eighteen hundred and fifty-six, twelve thousand five hundred dollars.

For interest on two hundred and fifty thousand dollars, at five per centaur, to be paid as annuity, (they having joined their brethren West), per eighth article treaty August seven, eighteen hundred and fifty-six, twelve thousand five hundred dollars

For interest on fifty thousand dollars, at the rate of five per centaur per annum, "to be paid annually for the support of schools," as per third article treaty of March twenty-one, eighteen hundred and sixty-six, two thousand five hundred dollars.

For interest on twenty thousand dollars, at the rate of five per centum per annum, "to be paid annually," for the support of the Seminole government, as per third article treaty of March twenty-one, eighteen hundred and sixty-six, one thousand dollars.

Senecas.—For permanent annuity in specie, per fourth article treaty September twenty-nine, eighteen hundred and seventeen, five hundred dollars.

For permanent annuity in specie, per fourth article treaty September seventeen, eighteen hundred and eighteen, five hundred dollars.

For blacksmith and assistant, shops and tools, iron and steel, to be applied as stipulated in seventh article treaty of February twenty-three, eighteen hundred and sixty-seven, one thousand and sixty dollars.

For miller, during the pleasure of the President, six hundred dollars.

Senecas of New York.—For permanent annuity, in lieu of interest on stock, per act of February nineteen, eighteen and thirty-one, six thousand dollars.

For interest, in lieu of investment, on seventy-five thousand dollars, at five per centum, per act of June twenty-seven, eighteen hundred and forty-three thousand seven hundred and fifty dollars.

For interest, at five per centum, on forty-three thousand and fifty dollars, transferred from the Ontario Bank to the United States treasury, per act of June twenty-seven, eighteen hundred and forty-six, two thousand one hundred and fifty-two dollars and fifty cents.

Senecas and Shawnees.—For permanent annuity, in specie, per fourth article treaty September seventeen, eighteen hundred and eighteen, one thousand dollars

For blacksmith and assistant, shop and tools, iron and steel, ante thousand and sixty dollars.

Senecas, Mixed Senecas, and Shawnees, Quapaws, Confederated Peorias, Kaskaskias, Weas, and Piankeshaws, Ottawas of Blanchard's Fork, and Roche de Bœuf, and certain Wyandotts.—For third of five instalments for blacksmith and assistant, shop and tools, iron and steel for shop for Shawnees, five hundred dollars.

For, third of six instalments for pay of blacksmith, and for necessary airon and steel and tools for Peorias, Kaskaskias, Wean, and Piankeshaws, one thousand one hundred and twenty-three dollars and twenty-nine and cents.

Shawnees.—For permanent annuity for educational purposes, per fourth articles treaty August three, seventeen hundred and ninety-five, and third article treaty May ten, eighteen hundred and fifty-four, one thousand dollars.

For permanent annuity, in specie, for educational purposes, per fourth article treaty September twenty-nine, eighteen hundred and seventeen, and third article treaty may ten, eighteen hundred and my four, two thousand dollars.

For interest, at five per centum, on forty thousand dollars, for educational purposes, per third article treaty May ten, eighteen hundred and fifty-four, two thousand dollars.

Shoshones

EASTERN BANDS.—FOR EIGHTH OF TWENTY instalments, to be expended, under the direction of the President, in the purchase of such articles as he may deem suitable to their wants, either as hunters or herdsmen, per fifth article treaty July two, eighteen hundred and sixty-three, ten thousand dollars.

Western Bands.—For eighth of twenty instalments, to be expended, Western bands under the direction of the President, in the purchase of such articles as he may deem suitable to their wants, either as bunters or herdsmen, per seventh article treaty October one, eighteen hundred and sixty-three, five thousand dollars.

Northwestern Bands.—For eighth of twenty instalments, to be expended, under the direction of the President, in the purchase of such articles as he may deem suitable to their wants, either as hunters or herdsmen, per third article treaty July thirty, eighteen hundred and sixty-three, five thousand dollars.

Goship Band.—For eighth of twenty instalments, to be expended, under direction of the President, in the purchase of such articles, including cattle for herding or other purposes, as he shall deem suitable to their wants and condition as hunters or herdsmen, cm thousand dollars.

Shoshones and Bannocks

SHOSHONES.—FOR FIRST OF THREE INSTALMENTS for the purchase of seed and implements to the heads of families or lodges who shall continue to farm (say one hundred families), two thousand five hundred dollars.

For second of thirty instalments to purchase eight hundred suits of clothing for pastes over fourteen years of age, the flannel, hoe, calico, and domestics for eight hundred females over the age of twelve years, and such goods as may be needed to make suits for eight hundred boys and girls, thirteen thousand eight hundred and seventy-four dollars.

For first of ten instalments for the purchase of such articles as may be considered proper by the Secretary of the Interior for one thousand eight hundred persons roaming, and six hundred persons engaged in agriculture, thirty thousand dollars.

For pay of physician, teacher, carpenter, engineer, farmer, and blacksmith, as per tenth article treaty July three, eighteen hundred and sixty-eight, six thousand eight hundred dollars.

For first of three instalments to be expended in presents or the ten persons who grow the most valuable crops, under same act and treaty, five hundred dollars.

For pay of second blacksmith and furnishing iron and steel and other materials, under same article of said treaty, two thousand dollars.

Bannocks.—For second of thirty instalments to purchase four hundred suits of clothing for males over fourteen years of age, the flannel, hose, calico, and domestics for four hundred females over the age of twelve years, and such flannel and cotton goods as may be needed, to make suits for four hundred boys and girls, six thousand nine hundred and thirty-seven dollars.

For second of ten instalments for the purchase of such articles as may be considered proper by the Secretary of the Interior for eight hundred persons roaming, and four hundred persons engaged in agriculture, sixteen thousand dollars.

For purchase of seeds and agricultural implements to be furnished the heads of families or lodges who dire to commence farming, ten thousand dollars.

For pay of physician, teacher, carpenter, engineer, farmer, and black, smith, six thousand eight hundred dollars.

For second of three instalments, to be expended in presents for the ten persons who grow the most valuable crops, five hundred dollars.

For transportation of goods that may be purchased for the Shoshones and Bannocks, fifteen thousand dollars.

Shoshones and Bannocks, and other Bands of Idaho and Southeastern Oregon.—For this amount, to be expended in such goods, provisions, or Idaho and of other articles as the President may from time to time determine, including insurance and transportation thereof; in instructing in agricultural pursuits; in providing employees, educating children, procuring medicine and medical attendance; car for and support of the aged, sick, and infirm; for the helpless orphans of said Indians; and in any other respect to promote their civilization, comfort, and improvement, forty thousand dollars.

Six Nations of New York.—For permanent annuity in clothing and other useful articles, per sixth article treat November *seventeen* (eleven), seventeen hundred and ninety-four, four thousand five hundred dollars.

Sioux of different Tribes, including Santee Sioux in the State of Nebraska.—For the erection of a steam circular saw-mill, with grist-mill and shingle-machine attached, eight thousand dollars.

For first of three instalments for purchase of seeds and implements to be furnished heads of families or lodges (say six hundred), fifteen thousand dollars.

For pay of second blacksmith, and furnishing iron, steel, and other material, two thousand dollars.

For second of thirty instalments to purchase clothing for males over fourteen years of age, for flannel, hose, calico, and domestics required for females over twelve years of age; and for such flannel and cotton goods as may be needed to make suits for boys and girls, one hundred and fifty-nine thousand four hundred dollars.

For second of thirty instalments to purchase such articles as may be considered proper by the Secretary of the Interior for persons roaming and for persons engaged in agriculture, two hundred and thirty-six thousand dollars.

For second of four instalments for purchase of beef and flour, under tenth article treaty of April twenty-nine, eighteen hundred and sixty-eight, and for subsistence of Yankton Sioux, one million three hundred and fourteen thousand dollars.

For pay of physician, five teachers, one carpenter, one miller, one engineer, one farmer, and one blacksmith, ten thousand four hundred dollars.

For second of three instalments, to be expended in presents to the ten persons who grow the most valuable crops, five hundred dollars.

For insurance, transportation, and the necessary expenses of delivering goods to be purchased for the different bands of the Sioux Indians, under treaty of April twenty-ninth, eighteen hundred and Sixty-eight, seventy-five thousand dollars.

Sisseton and Wahpeton and flames Sioux of Lake Traverse and Devil's Lake.—For this amount, to be expended in such goods, provisions, or other articles as the President may from time to time determine, including insurance and transportation thereof, in instructing in agricultural and mechanical pursuits, in providing employees, educating children, procuring medicine and medical attendance, care for and support of the aged, sick, and infirm, for the helpless orphans of said Indians, and in any other respect to promote their civilization, comfort, and improvement, seventy-five thousand dollars.

S'Klallams.—For second of five instalments on sixty thousand dollars, (being the fifth series), under the direction of the

President, per fifth article treaty January twenty-six, eighteen, hundred and fifty-five, two thousand four hundred dollars.

For twelfth of twenty instalments for the support of an agricultural and industrial school, and, for pay-for suitable teachers, per eleventh article treaty October (January) twenty-six, eighteen hundred and fifty-five, two thousand five hundred dollars.

For twelfth of twenty instalments for the employment of a blacksmith, carpenter, farmer, and a physician, who shall furnish medicine for the sick, per treaty June (January) twenty-six, eighteen hundred and fifty-five, tour thousand six hundred dollars.

For support of a smith and carpenter shop, and to provide the necessary tools therefor, five hundred dollars.

Tabeguache Band of Utah Indians.—For the eighth of ten instalments for the purchase of goods, under the direction of the Secretary of the Interior, per eighth article treaty of October seven, eighteen hundred and sixty-three, and Senate amendment of March twenty-five, eighteen hundred and sixty-four, ten thousand dollars. For the eighth of ten instalments, per eighth article of said treaty, for the purchase of provisions, under the direction of the Secretary of the Interior, ten thousand dollars.

For the purchase of iron, steel, and tools necessary for blacksmith's shop, as per tenth article of said treaty, two hundred and twenty dollars.

For pay of blacksmith and assistant, as per same article of same treaty, one thousand one hundred dollars.

For insurance, transportation, and general incidental expenses of the delivery of goods, provisions, and stock, as per same article of same treaty, two thousand dollars.

Tabeguache, Muache, Capote, Weeminuche, Yampa, Grand River, and Uintah Bands of Utes.—For pay of two carpenters, two millers, two farmers, and one blacksmith, as per fifteenth article treaty of March two, eighteen hundred and sixty-eight, nine thousand dollars.

For pay of two teachers, per, same article, two thousand dollars.

For the purchase of iron and steel, and the necessary tools for blacksmith's shop, two hundred and twenty dollars.

For third of thirty instalments, to be expended under the direction of the Secretary of the Interior, for clothing, blankets, 'and such other articles as he may think proper and necessary, under eleventh article of same treaty, thirty thousand dollars.

For annual amount, to be expended under the direction of the Secretary of the Interior, in supplying said Indiana with beef, mutton, wheat, flour, beans, and potatoes, as per twelfth article same treaty, thirty thousand dollars.

For insurance and transportation of goods as may be purchased for said Indiana, seven thousand five hundred dollars.

Umpquas (Cow Creek Band).—For eighteenth of twenty instalments in blankets, clothing, provisions, and stock, per third article treaty September nineteen, eighteen hundred and fifty-three, five hundred and fifty dollars

Umpquas and Calapooias of Umpqua Valley, Oregon.—For second of five instalments of the fourth series of annuity for beneficial objects, to be expended as directed by the President, per third article treaty November twenty-nine, eighteen hundred and fifty-four, one thousand dollars.

For seventeenth of twenty instalments for the pay of a teacher and purchase of books and stationery, per sixth article treaty November twenty-nine, eighteen hundred and My-four, one thousand four hundred and My dollars.

Wichitas, and other affiliated Bands, and Indians in Country leased from Choctaws.—For this amount, to be expended in such goods, proaty visions, and other articles as the President may from time to time determine, including insurance and transportation thereof, in instructing in agricultural and mechanical pursuits, in providing employees, educating children, procuring medicine and medical attendance, care and support of the aged, sick, and infirm, for the helpless orphans of said Indians, and in any other respect to promote their civilization, comfort, and improvement, forty thousand dollars.

Walla-Walla, Cayuse, and Umatilla Tribes.—For second of five instalments of third series, to be expended under the direction of the President, per second article treaty June nine, eighteen hundred and fifty-five, four thousand dollars.

For twelfth of twenty instalments for the purchase of all necessary mill fixtures and mechanical tools, medicines, and hospital stores, books and stationery for schools, repairs of school building, and furniture, and for employees, three thousand dollars.

For twelfth of twenty instalments for the pay and subsistence of one superintendent of farming operations, one farmer, two millers, one black smith, one wagon and plow maker, one carpenter and joiner, one physician, and two teachers, per fourth article treaty June nine, eighteen hundred and fifty-five, eleven thousand two hundred dollars.

For twelfth of twenty instalments for the pay of each of the head chiefs of the Walla-Walla, Cayuse, and Umatilla bands, the sum of five hundred dollars per annum, per fifth article treaty June nine, eighteen hundred and fifty-five, one thousand five hundred dollars.

Winnebagoes.—For interest on eight hundred and ninety five thousand four hundred and ninety-three dollars and fifteen cents, at five per centum, per fourth article treaty November one, eighteen hundred and thirty-seven, and joint resolution July seventeen, eighteen hundred and sixty-two, four thousand seven hundred and seventy-four dollars and sixty-six cents.

For twenty-fifth of thirty instalments of interest on seventy-six thou sand one hundred and sixteen dollars and ninety-two cents, at five per centum, per fourth article treaty October thirteen, eighteen hundred and forty-six, three thousand eight hundred and five d and eighty-four cents.

For interest on one hundred and seventy-nine thousand and ninety-eight dollars and sixty-three cents, at five per centum, to be expended under the direction of the Secretary of the Interior, for the erection of houses, improvement of their allotments of land, purchase of stock, agricultural implements, seeds, and other beneficial purposes, eight thousand nine hundred and fifty-four dollars and ninety-three cents.

For the proportion of one hundred and sixty persons of one million dollars, placed to the credit of said Indians on the books e§ the treasury, as per fourth article of the treaty November one, eighteen hundred and thirty-seven, whole number of the tribe being one thousand five hundred and thirty-one persons, one hundred and four thousand five hundred and six dollars and eighty-five cents.

For the proportion of one hundred and sixty persons of eighty-five thousand dollars, placed to the credit of said Indians on the books of the treasury, as per fourth article treaty October thirteen, eighteen hundred and forty-six, whole number one thousand five hundred and thirty-one, eight thousand eight hundred and eighty-three dollars and eight cents.

For the proportion of one hundred and sixty persons of two hundred thousand dollars, placed to the credit of said Indians on the books of the treasury, being the amount in part taken from their tribal funds to pay the expenses of their removal from Minnesota, provided for in public act number one hundred and eighty-seven, approved July fifteen, eighteen hundred and seventy, whole number one thousand five hundred and thirty-one, twenty thousand nine hundred and one dollars and thirty-seven cents. The foregoing amounts for said one hundred and sixty persons are appropriated from the sums respectively named standing to the credit of the Winnebagoes on the books of the treasury, and shall be deducted therefrom.

For insurance and transportation of goods that may be purchased for said Indians, one thousand five hundred dollars.

Wall-pah-pee Tribe of Snake Indians.—For last of five instalments, to be expended under the direction of the President, as per seventh article treaty of August twelve, eighteen hundred and sixty-five, two thousand dollars.

Yakama Nation.—For first of two instalments of third series for beneficial objects, under the direction of the President, per fourth article treaty June nine, eighteen hundred and fifty-five, five, six thousand dollars.

For twelfth of twenty instalments for the support of two schools, one of which is to be an agricultural and industrial school, keeping in repair school buildings, and for providing suitable furniture, books, and stationery, per fifth article treaty June nine, eighteen hundred and fifty-five, five hundred dollars.

For twelfth of twenty instalments for the employment, of one superintendent of teaching and two teachers, per fifth article treaty June nine, eighteen hundred and fifty-five, three thousand two hundred dollars.

For twelfth of twenty instalments for the employment of one superintendent of farming and two farmers, two millers, two blacksmiths, one tinner, one gunsmith, one carpenter, and one wagon and plow maker, per fifth article of treaty of June nine, eighteen hundred and fifty-five, eleven thousand four hundred dollars.

For twelfth of twenty instalments for keeping in repair saw and flouring mills, and for furnishing the necessary tools and fixtures, per fifth article treaty June nine, eighteen hundred and fifty-five, five hundred dollars.

For twelfth of twenty instalments for keeping in repair the hospital and providing the necessary medicines and fixtures therefor, per fifth article treaty June nine, eighteen hundred and fifty five, three hundred dollars.

For twelfth of twenty instalments for keeping in repair blacksmith's, tinsmith's, gunsmith's, carpenter's, and wagon and plow maker's shops, and for providing necessary tools therefor, per fifth article treaty June nine, eighteen hundred and fifty-five, five hundred dollars.

For twelfth of twenty instalments for the pay of a physician, per fifth article treaty June nine, eighteen hundred and fifty-five, one thousand two hundred dollars.

For twelfth of twenty instalments for keeping in repair the buildings required for the various employees, and for providing the necessary furniture therefor, per fifth article treaty June nine, eighteen hundred and fifty five, three hundred dollars.

For twelfth of twenty instalments for the salary of such person as the said confederated tribes and bands of Indians may select to be their head chief, per fifth article treaty June nine, eighteen hundred and fifty-five, five hundred dollars.

Yankton Tribe of Sioux.—For third of ten instalments, (second of series), to be paid to them or expended, for their benefit, commencing with the year in which they shall remove to and settle and reside upon their reservation, per fourth article treaty April nineteen, eighteen hundred and fifty-eight, forty thousand dollars.

For insurance and transportation of goods for the Yanktons, one thousand five hundred dollars: *Provided*, That hereafter no Indian nation or tribe within the territory of the United States shall be acknowledged or be recognized as an independent nation, tribe, or power with whom the United States may contract by treaty: *Provided, further*, That nothing herein contained shall be construed to invalidate or impair the obligation of any treaty heretofore lawfully made and ratified with any such Indian nation or tribe.

General Incidental Expenses of the Indian Service

ARIZONA.—FOR THE GENERAL INCIDENTAL EXPENSES of the Indian service in the Territory of Arizona, presents of goods, agricultural implements, and other useful articles, and to assist them to locate in permanent abodes, and sustain themselves by the pursuits of civilized life, to be expended under the direction of the Secretary of the Interior, seventy thousand dollars.

California.—For the general incidental expenses of the Indian service in California, pay of employees, presents of goods, agricultural implements, and other useful articles, and to assist them to locate in permanent abodes, and sustain themselves by the pursuits of civilized life, to be expended under the direction of the Secretary of the Interior, seventy-five thousand dollars.

Colorado Territory.—For the general incidental expenses of Indian service in Colorado Territory, presents of goods, agricultural implements, and other useful articles, and to assist them to locate in permanent abodes, and sustain themselves by the pursuits of civilized life, to be expended under the direction of the Secretary of the Interior, twenty thousand dollars.

Dakota Territory.—For the general incidental expenses of the Indian service in Dakota Territory, presents of goods, agricultural implements, and other useful articles, and to assist them to locate in permanent abodes, and sustain themselves by the pursuits of civilized life, to be expended under the direction of the Secretary of the Interior, twenty thousand dollars.

Idaho Territory.—For the general incidental expenses of the Indian service in Idaho Territory, presents of goods, agricultural implements, and other useful articles, and to assist them to locate in permanent abodes, and sustain themselves by the pursuits of civilized life, to be expended under the direction off the Secretary of the Interior, twenty thousand dollars.

Montana Territory.—For the general incidental expenses of the Indian service in Montana Territory, presents of goods, agricultural implements, and other useful articles, and to assist them to locate in permanent abodes, and to sustain themselves by the pursuits of civilized life, to be expended under the direction of the Secretary of the Interior, fifteen thousand dollars.

Nevada.—For the general incidental expenses of the Indian service in Nevada, presents of goods, agricultural implements, and other useful articles, and to assist them to locate in permanent abodes, and sustain themselves by the pursuits of civilized life, to be expended under the direction of the Secretary of the Interior, fifteen thousand dollars.

New Mexico.—For the general incidental expenses of the Indian service in New Mexico, presents of goods, agricultural implements, and other useful articles, and to assist them to locate in permanent abodes, anal sustain themselves by the pursuits of civilized life, to be expended under the direction of the Secretary of the Interior, fifty thousand dollars, including five thousand dollars to be expended in establishing schools among the Pueblo Indians.

Oregon.—For the general incidental expenses of the Indian service in Oregon, including insurance and transportation of annuity goods and presents, (where no special provision therefor is made by treaties), and for defraying the expenses of the removal and subsistence of Indians in Oregon, (not parties to any treaty), and for pay of necessary employees, forty thousand dollars.

For this amount, to survey and allot lands in severalty to the Indians at Grande Ronde reservation in Oregon, who may desire and be fitted for the same, under the provisions of the treaty of January twenty-second, eighteen hundred and fifty-flue, with the confederate bands of Indians residing in Willamette Valley, the title thereto not to be alienated by said Indium without the consent of the Secretary of the Interior, four thousand dollars.

For repairs at Grande Ronde agency, two thousand dollars.

Washington Territory.—For the general incidental expenses of the Washington Indian service in Washington Territory, and for defraying the expenses of removal and subsistence of Indians, (not parties to any treaty), and for pay of necessary employees, twenty-four thousand four hundred dollars *Provided,* That the balance not expended as herein provided shall be expended in the establishment of schools and the education of Indian children in said Territory.

Utah Territory.—For the general incidental expenses of the Indian service in Utah Territory, presents of goods, agricultural implements, and other useful articles, and to assist them to locate in permanent abodes, and sustain themselves by the pursuits of civilized life, to be expended under the direction of the Secretary of the Interior, fifteen thousand dollars.

For this amount, to carry out the action contemplated by act of Congress approved May live, eighteen hundred and sixty-four, entitled "An act to vacate and sell the present Indian reservations in Utah Territory, and to settle said Indians in Uintah Valley," ten thousand dollars.

Wyoming Territory.—For the general incidental expenses of the Indian service in Wyoming Territory, presents of goods, agricultural implements, and other articles, and to assist them to locate in permanent abodes, and sustain themselves by the pursuits of civilized life, to be expended under the direction of the Secretary of the Interior, twenty thousand dollars.

For transportation, and necessary expenses of the delivery of annum in ties and provisions to the Indian tribes in Minnesota and Michigan, ten thousand dollars.

For this amount, or so much thereof as may be necessary, to pay the expenses of the commission of citizens serving without pay, appointed by the President under the provisions of the fourth section of the act of April ten, eighteen hundred and sixty-nine, the sum of fifteen thousand dollars; and said commission is hereby continued with the powers and duties heretofore provided by law: *Provided,* That hereafter no payments shall be by any officer of the United States to contractors for goods or supplies of any sort furnished to the Indians, or for the transportation thereon, or for any buildings or machinery erected or placed on their reservations, under or by virtue of any contract entered into with the Interior Department, or any branch thereof, on the receipts or certificates of the Indian agents or superintendents for such supplies, goods, transportation, buildings, or machinery beyond fifty percent of the amount due until the accounts and vouchers shall have been submitted to the executive committee the board of commissioners appointed by the President of the United States, and organized under the provisions of the fourth section of the act April tenth, eighteen hundred and sixty-nine, and the third section of the act approved *April* (July) fifteenth, eighteen hundred and seventy, for examination, revisal, and approval; and it shall be the duty of said board of commissioners, without unnecessary delay, to forward said accounts and vouchers so submitted to them to the Secretary of the Interior, with the reasons for their approval or disapproval of the same, in whole or in part, attached thereto; and said Secretary shall hare power to sustain, set aside, or modify the action of said board, and cause payment to be made or withheld as he may determine.

For this amount, or so much thereof as may be necessary, for the purchase of provisions for Red Cloud's band of Sioux Indians, to relieve their present wants, and to subsist them until July first, eighteen hundred and seventy-one, one hundred and sixty-five thousand dollars: *Provided*, That so much of the amount hereby appropriated as may be necessary shall be used to reimburse the subsistence department for supplies furnished by that department, under the direction of the President of January twenty-third, eighteen hundred and seventy-one.

For this amount, to carry on the work of instructing and aiding the Indians of the central superintendency in the arts of civilization with a view to their self-support, to be expended under the direction of the Secretary of the Interior, forty thousand dollars, or so much thereof as he may deem necessary.

The Secretary of the Interior is hereby authorized to defray the expenses of delegations of Indians visiting the city of Washington by authority of the United States, subsequently to the first day of January, eighteen hundred and seventy-one, and to purchase presents for the members thereof, out of the amount remaining unexpended on the thin-first day of December, eighteen hundred and seventy, of the sum fifty thousand dollars appropriated by resolution number one hundred and ten, entitled "A resolution to pay expenses of delegations of Indians visiting the city of Washington," approved July fifteenth, eighteen hundred and seventy; and tine paragraph of the act entitled "An act making appropriations for the current and contingent expenses of the Indian department, and for fulfilling treaty stipulations with various Indian tribes, for the year ending June thirty, eighteen hundred and seventy-one, and for other purposes," approved holy fifteenth, eighteen hundred and seventy, which is as follows, viz: "For this amount, or so Amendment much thereof as may be necessary for subsistence of the Navajos Indians in New Mexico, for the year ending June thirty, eighteen hundred and seventy, to be expended under the direction of the Secretary of the Interior, seventy-five thousand dollars," be, and the same is hereby, amended by striking out the words "eighteen hundred and seventy," and inserting in lieu thereof the words "eighteen hundred and seventy-one."

For this amount, to enable the Secretary of the Interior to pay Alvin N. Blacklidge for services rendered and money expended in taking the census of the Cherokee Indians, under the provisions of the twelfth article of the treaty of eighteen hundred and sixty-six, with said Indians, nine hundred and thirty-eight dollars and fifty-five cents.

For this amount, or so much thereof as may be necessary, for the removal of the Kiokapoo and other American Indian tribes roving on the borders of Mexico and Texas to reservations within the Territories of the United States, and for their settlement and subsistence on such reservations, forty thousand dollars.

For this amount, or so much thereof as may be necessary, to enable the Secretary of the Interior to cause settlements to be made with all persons appointed by Indian councils, to receive money due incompetent or orphan Indians, per act of July five, eighteen hundred and sixty-two, (Statutes at Large, volume twelve, pages five hundred and twenty-nine and five hundred and thirty), five thousand dollars.

For surveying such reservations in Oregon, under treaty stipulations, as may be rendered necessary, twenty thousand dollars.

For the erection or purchase, at the discretion of the Secretary of the Interior, of suitable buildings for the Upper Missouri agency, near Fort Upper Berthold, provided the same shall be necessary, eight thousand dollars.

For this amount, or so much thereof as may be necessary, to defray he expenses of determining the location and re-marking with suitable monuments and establishing the position of the ninety-sixth meridian west longitude, from the State of Kansas to the north line of the Creek country, in the Indian Territory, five thousand dollars; and this amount, Expenses of or so much thereof as may be necessary to pay the expenses of holding general council. a "general council" of the Cherokee, Creek, Seminole, and Choctaw and Chickasaw Indians, in the Indian Territory, as provided by the treaties with said tribes in eighteen hundred and sixty-six, for the fiscal year ending June thirty, eighteen hundred and seventy two, thirteen thousand five hundred dollars: *Provided*, That any other Indian tribe permanently located in said Indian Territory shall be, and is hereby, authorized to elect and send to said "general council" one delegate, and in addition one delegate for each one thousand Indians or fraction of a thousand greater than five hundred, being members of such tribe, on the same terms and conditions, and with the same rights and privileges, including right to compensation, as is provided for delegates of the tribes hereinbefore mentioned, and a sufficient sum to pay the per diem and mileage of such additional delegates is hereby appropriated.

Interest on Trust-Fund Stocks.—For payment of interest on certain abstracted and non-paying State stocks belonging to various Indian tribes, (and held in trust by the Secretary of the Interior), for the fiscal year ending June thirty, eighteen hundred and seventy-one, viz.:—

For interest on the Cherokee national fund, eighteen thousand nine hundred and eighty dollars.

For interest on the Cherokee school farad, three thousand and ten dollars.

For interest on the Chickasaw national find, fifteen thousand one hundred and forty dollars.

For interest on the Chickasaw incompetents' fund, two hundred dollars.

For interest on the Choctaw general fund, twenty-seven thousand dollars.

For interest on the Creek orphans' fund, five thousand two hundred Creeks; and eighteen dollars.

For interest on the Delaware general fund, nine thousand seven hundred and ten dollars.

For interest on the Iowas' fund, three thousand three hundred and forty dollars.

For interest on the Kaskaskias, Weas, Peorias, and Piankeshaws' fund, six thousand and seventy dollars.

For interest on the Menomonees' fund, nine hundred and fifty dollars.

For interest on the Ottawas and Chippewas, two hundred and thirty Ottawa and dollars.

For interest on the Pottawatomies' education fund, six thousand seven hundred dollars.

For contingent expenses of trust funds, heretofore and to be hereafter incurred, three thousand dollars; and the Secretary of the Treasury is Bounds to hereby authorized to issue to the Choctaw tribe of Indiana bonds of the United States to the amount of two hundred and fifty thousand dollars, as directed by the act of March two, eighteen hundred and sixty-one, entitled "An act making appropriations for the current and contingent expenses of the Indian department, and for fulfilling treaty stipulations with various Indian tribes."

Sec 2. That the act, approved July fifteen, eighteen hundred and seventy, "making appropriations for the current and contingent expenses of the Indian department, and for fulfilling treaty stipulations with various Indian tribes, for the year ending

June thirty, eighteen hundred *and* seventy-one, and for other purposes, amended by adding the following section, which was inadvertently omitted in the enrolment of said act, viz.:—

"SEC. 14. *And be it further enacted*, That nothing in this act contained, or in any of the provisions thereof, shall be so construed as to ratify, approve, or disaffirm any treaty made with any tribes, bands, or parties of Indiana since the twentieth of July, eighteen hundred and sixty-seven, or affirm or disaffirm any of the powers of the Executive and Senate over the subject."

SEC 3. That hereafter no contract or agreement of any kind shall be made with made by any person, with any tribe of Indians, or individual Indian not a citizen of the United States, for the payment of any money or other thing of value to him, or any other person, in consideration of services for said Indians relative to their lands, or to any claims growing out of or in reference to annuities from or treaties with the United States, unless such contract or agreement be in writing and approved by the commissioner of Indian affairs and the Secretary of the Interior; and all such contracts or agreements hereafter made, in violation of the provisions of this section, are hereby declared null and void, and all making may be money or other thing of value paid to any person by any Indian or tribe, or anyone else, for or on his or their behalf, on account of such services, in excess of the amount approved by the said commissioner and Secretary for such services, may be recovered by suit in the name of the United States in any court of the United States, regardless of the amount in controversy, one half of which shall be paid to the person suing for the same, and the other half shall be paid into the treasury of the United States, for the use of the Indian or tribe by or for whom it was so paid; and the person so receiving said money, and his aiders and abettors, shall, in addition to the forfeiture of said sum, be subject to prosecution for misdemeanor in any court of the United States, and on conviction shall be fined not less than sue thousand dollars, and imprisoned not less than six months, and it shall be the duty of all district attorneys of the United States to prosecute such cases when applied to do so, and their failure and refusal shall be ground for their removal from office.

And any Indian agent, or other person in the employment of the United States, who shall, in violation of the provisions of this section, advise, sanction, or in anyway aid in the making of such contracts or agreements, or in making such payments as are here prohibited, shall, in addition to the punishment herein imposed on the person making said contract, or receiving said money, be, on conviction, dismissed from the service of the United States, and be forever disqualified from holding any office of profit or trust under the same.

APPROVED, March 8, 1871.

A Note About the Author

Ten Documents That Created America contains ten documents written by the Founding Fathers of the United States including John Jay, Benjamin Franklin, and Robert R. Livingston; The Constitutional Convention including James Madison and Alexander Hamilton; The 1st United States Congress including John Adams; several presidents of the United States such as Abraham Lincoln and Andrew Jackson; Union General Gordon Granger; and the formerly enslaved African-American abolitionist and orator, Frederick Douglass.

Note from the Publisher

Since our inception in 2020, Mint Editions has kept sustainability and innovation at the forefront of our mission. Each and every Mint Edition title gets a fresh, professionally typeset manuscript and a dazzling new cover, all while maintaining the integrity of the original book. With thousands of titles in our collection, we aim to spotlight diverse public domain works to help them find modern audiences. Mint Editions celebrates a breadth of literary works, curated from both canonical and overlooked classics from writers around the globe.

bookfinity & MINT EDITIONS

Enjoy more of your favorite classics with Bookfinity,
a new search and discovery experience for readers.
With Bookfinity, you can discover more vintage
literature for your collection, find your Reader Type,
track books you've read or want to read,
and add reviews to your favorite books.
Visit www.bookfinity.com, and click on
Take the Quiz to get started.

Don't forget to follow us
@bookfinityofficial and @mint_editions

www.ingramcontent.com/pod-product-compliance
Lightning Source LLC
Chambersburg PA
CBHW031442040426
42444CB00007B/934